Affirmations of God and man

Books by EDMUND FULLER

A Pageant of the Theatre
John Milton
A Star Pointed North *(novel)*
Brothers Divided *(novel)*
George Bernard Shaw: *Critic of Western Morale*
Vermont: *A History of the Green Mountain State*
Tinkers and Genius: *The Story of the Yankee Inventors*
Man in Modern Fiction
Books With Men Behind Them
The Corridor *(novel)*
Successful Calamity

Affirmations
of
God and man

writings for modern dialogue

EDITED BY EDMUND FULLER

ASSOCIATION PRESS / NEW YORK

AFFIRMATIONS OF GOD AND MAN

Acknowledgments

We wish to thank the following publishers for kind permission to quote from
copyrighted material. If by accident any proper acknowledgment is omitted,
or necessary permission unobtained, we express sincere regret and the desire
to rectify the matter as opportunity permits. All material is credited to author
and source in the text. The sources of many are listed in the bibliography.

The University of Chicago Press for excerpts from Paul Tillich: *Biblical Re-
ligion and the Search for Ultimate Reality,* copyright© 1955 by U. of Chi. Press;
Farrar, Straus & Giroux, Inc. for excerpts from Abraham Joshua Heschel: *God
in Search of Man,* copyright© 1955 by A. J. Heschel, from Thomas Merton:
Seasons of Celebration, copyright 1950,© 1958, 1962, 1964, 1965 by The Abbey
of Gethsemani; Harcourt, Brace & World, Inc. for excerpts from C. S. Lewis:
Surprised by Joy and *The World's Last Night,* copyright© 1955, 1959 by C. S.
Lewis, from T. S. Eliot: *Murder in the Cathedral,* copyright 1935 by HB&W,
Inc., copyright© 1963 by T. S. Eliot, from Robert Elliott Fitch: *Odyssey of the
Self-Centered Self,* copyright© 1960, 1961 by R. E. Fitch; Harper & Row, Publishers, Inc. for excerpts from pp. 137–40 of Romain Gary: *The Ski Bum,* copy-
right© 1964, 1965 by Romain Gary, from Martin Buber: *Eclipse of God,*
copyright 1952 by Harper & Row, Inc., from Chad Walsh: *Behold the Glory,*
copyright© 1955–56 by Chad Walsh, from Martin C. D'Arcy: *No Absent God,*
copyright© 1962 by Martin C. D'Arcy, from Jacques Maritain: *Approaches to
God,* copyright 1952 by Harper & Row, Inc.; Louisiana State University Press
for excerpts from Russell Kirk: *The Intemperate Professor,* copyright© 1965
by the publisher; The Macmillan Co. for excerpts from Dietrich Bonhoeffer:
Creation and Fall and Temptation, copyright© 1959 by SCM Press Ltd., from
George Hedley: *Superstitions of the Irreligious,* copyright 1951 by the publisher; David McKay Co., Inc. for excerpts from Evelyn Underhill: *An Anthology of the Love of God,* copyright 1954 by the publisher; University of North

For

JOHN O. PATTERSON

Priest—Headmaster—Friend

Preface

This book approaches the Christian faith at those points where it faces some characteristic challenges of the present time. In an age in which, for a large number of articulate and influential persons, Christian belief is not the accepted premise of life, the first task of apologetics may be the awakening of the skeptical and the uninstructed to the fact that Christianity is something which not only merits but demands their attention. Has any believer failed to ask at some time, if only in his secret heart, "What if it isn't true?" The unbeliever who is honest should not fail to ask himself. "What if it *is* true?"

In the last few years I have taught theology at the secondary school level and have lectured on theological implications of modern literature at a number of colleges. Such work leads to give-and-take bull sessions with students—experiences which reveal the paradoxical coexistence of intense interest in, and equally intense resistance to, religion. Among students at both school and college we must engage spiritedly in a struggle for the commitment of minds, for in the process of secular education young men and women meet the massive array of presuppositions of our day that are hostile to Christianity and hear little or nothing of the Christian message.

From these encounters I have learned at least something of what is wanted and needed. Beyond all other aspects of Christian faith, student questions require us to discuss the *idea*—the basic concept—of God, of Man, and of Creation. Accordingly it is those three doctrines that are given primary attention in this book, though the material leads us on to other aspects of Christian thought and life.

This is a collection of brief statements, culled generally from longer works, about Christian belief and practice. The bibliography of source books comprises a diverse, stimulating program for further reading, and offers a basis for the systematic study of Christian doctrine that this book does not pretend to be.

Most of the writers are modern, contemporary with us, except that occasionally, venerated older voices chime in to remind us that nothing here is a novelty: either in question or in answer.

New voices today are asserting the old lie that God is dead; others proclaim man to be a mere animal whose life is absurd and meaningless; still others demand total authority for the state, which owns man rather than serves him, or say that science has dissolved religious belief and superseded it.

All these challenges meet tough response in the statements of the sinewy-minded men and women represented here. These replies are not a defense, but a confident evangel that places the secular challengers on the defensive.

The spokesmen represent several centuries, notwithstanding the prevailing contemporaneity. They include laymen, priests, theologians, philosophers, scientists, poets, and novelists. If their testimony does not attract you toward, or strengthen you in, the Christian religion—or any other in which God is worshiped—it may at least help you to see what religion you *do* have—for like every man you have a religion, an ultimate concern, dedication, or commitment of some sort, be it that of self, man, state, party, or the mere gratification of your body.

Inevitably these selections reflect the experience, thinking, and reading of the editor. The book is kept to moderate size lest it expand beyond usefulness. For where is it to stop? The resources for its expansion and extension are vast. Any other man would have chosen other materials; the editor could have gone on culling and sifting indefinitely, and is doomed to think again and again as he reads, remembers, and discovers, "I wish *that* had been put in." The testimony, the literature of the faith is broad and deep. I know only the shallows and the shores. Yet I know what has been clarifying and strengthening to me, and what has been useful and provocative to many students with whom I have wrestled about this subject—sometimes under the label of literature and sometimes under the label of theology. The collection cannot be definitive, but it is provocative. It cannot exhaust any inquiry, but it can start many. Though the book is small, it opens windows upon vastness.

It is not meant to be read at one sitting or in long stretches. It cannot be used to advantage that way, for its materials are so concentrated, often being the nucleus of thought from some much-expanded context, that they need to be absorbed, pondered, and discussed in smaller units. There is an order to the arrangement but not such as to require its use in sequence. Browsing is encouraged. Each item is intended to start thought.

It may be a paradoxical advantage to some of the questers and questioners who use this book that its editor is a layman, a convert (after a lapse from a Christian upbringing), and purely an amateur in theology. I have stood where the most unbelieving reader stands. I have felt the weight of disbelief and, more important, have felt the impact of just such incisive minds as speak to you from these pages, making it clear that the complacent assumptions of easy disbelief are less rational, more "superstitious," and more a mass of presuppositions than are the dogmas of Christian faith. Those who know least about, or have heard the most garbled versions of, Christianity, may react with surprise at what they find here: "Is *that* what it claims? Is *that* what it's all about?" The informed Christian—there are all too many uninformed ones—is apt to know what the nonbeliever thinks, for he hears it stated incessantly. The nonbeliever is likely to have appalling misconceptions of what Christianity is, says, and does. The simplest intellectual honesty demands of us all: Examine what Christian teaching actually is, so that you will know clearly what you believe or don't believe.

These collected statements in themselves are not likely to persuade the unbeliever. But they are openers—leads. They are resources for the believer in his own thinking or in dialogue with the skeptic. In any case, it is not that they persuade (classical doctrine teaches that conversion is the work of the Holy Spirit, not of man) but that they thrust forward observations from diverse spokesmen not easily dismissed by an open mind. I call these "witnesses." They are affirmations that cannot be proved as the word *proof* is understood by some and misunderstood by others. Their force is in their affirmation, their "proof" is in both the successes and failures of man's history.

In teaching I still find many young people convinced, or afraid, that science has destroyed or superseded Christianity. There is enough in this book to show that the notion rests upon a woeful ignorance of both science and Christianity.

One of my wisest counselors, Chad Walsh, who works in the colleges, believes that there the emphasis of doubters has shifted from "How can you prove it's true?" to such questions as "Even if it's true, what difference does it make?" or "How can I accept a ready-made system of belief? Each man must create himself, must create his own values."

"What difference does it make?" is a challenge that arises about far more than religion. It is not a question but an attitude—the sloth that Dorothy Sayers defines on page 66. It is the theme of John Hersey's neo-Faustian novel of college life today, *Too Far to Walk*. Insofar as it *is* ever an honest question, much in this book touches it.

"How can I accept a ready-made system of belief?" also receives answer here in several ways—first by the evidence that it is not "ready-made," that there is much that each man must create, decide, and answer for himself in his relations to God and man. But an honest questioner must not forget that in greater or lesser degrees, all his intellectual baggage comes to him in part as a "ready-made" system. The world did not begin with him, or his generation. Wisdom begins when experience teaches us the limitation of what we do by and for ourselves. The chapters called "The Idea of Man" and "The Secular Challenge" have particular, but not exclusive, bearing upon these problems.

Deliberately I have used nothing directly from or about the current "God is dead" fad, but the entire book speaks to that. Buber's concept of the "eclipse of God," and the biblical "famine . . . of hearing the words of the Lord" focus the question. I seldom like to call an opinion with which I disagree contemptible, but that is how I feel about that contradiction in terms, "Death-of-God theology." It is intellectually dishonest, especially in seminaries and from professed Christian spokesmen. It is a trick phrase to mask the death of belief in its proponents. It disguises the less-attention-getting assertion that God does not exist, for God understood as God in the Judeo-Christian revelation, cannot die. He *is* or he is *not*—and evermore shall be.

Theodore Roethke says in his poem "The Decision": "Running from God's the longest race of all." Do we not all run it—we who try to know, love, and fear him, along with those who try to deny him? This book is not addressed by a complacent believer to unbelievers. Where there is no faith, may it help kindle it. Where there is faith, may it strengthen it. I hope by God's grace it may help any reader as much as gathering its materials has helped me.

It is a scandal but no secret that Christendom is divided in numerous ways. Some of the most dramatic historic events of recent years, capturing the attention of unbelievers and people of other religions as well as Christians, have sprung from the surging ecumenical spirit in Christendom. The late Pope John XXIII and the work of Vatican Council II and Pope Paul VI have been at the heart of this. Nothing in Christian doctrine promises that all differences will ever be resolved in the Church on Earth, but the new love and unity, even so far, lend strength and thrust to a faith and an institution (the whole Church) that some had said were moribund.

This book contains the voices of Roman Catholics, Anglicans, Protestants of several denominations, Jews, and two eminent unbelievers. As a book it expresses no sect or branch, but is simply Christian.

It does not encourage the dangerous notion of winning people to the faith by explaining the faith away, disclaiming its mysteries. Christianity *is* hard, it is still the "stumbling block" and "foolishness" that St. Paul said it was to some. As Dorothy Sayers says, page 31, "If all men are offended because of Christ, let them be offended; but where is the sense of their being offended at something that is not Christ and is nothing like Him? We do Him singularly little honor by watering down His personality till it could not offend a fly."

Some magnificent minds speak to us here. But as they remind us of, or first disclose to the unknowing, the intellectual force of religious thought, let none of us flatter ourselves that either our belief or disbelief is the fruit of our superior intelligence. Whoever we are, and whatever our bent of mind, from the arts to the sciences, we can find someone of greater intelligence, learning, or achievement than ourselves who believes or disbelieves. This proves that intelligence, intellectuality, per se, is not the cause of belief or unbelief. Belief is the fruit of grace interacting with will—of our commitment and God's aid.

Rome, Italy, and   Edmund Fuller
Kent, Connecticut

Contents

Batter my heart, three-personed God; for You
As yet but knock, breathe, shine, and seek to mend;
That I may rise, and stand, o'erthrow me, and bend
Your force, to break, blow, burn, and make me new.
I, like an usurped town to another due,
Labor to admit You, but oh! to no end;
Reason, Your viceroy in me, me should defend,
But is captived and proves weak or untrue.
Yet dearly I love You, and would be lovèd fain,
But am betrothed unto Your enemy.
Divorce me, untie, or break that knot again,
Take me to You, imprison me, for I
Except You enthrall me, never shall be free;
Nor ever chaste, except You ravish me.

JOHN DONNE

The Idea of God

"God" **is** the most heavy-laden of all human words. None has become so soiled, so mutilated. Just for this reason I may not abandon it. Generations of men have laid the burden of their anxious lives upon this word and weighed it to the ground; it lies in the dust and bears their whole burden. The races of man with their religious factions have torn the word to pieces; they have killed for it and died for it, and it bears their finger-marks and their blood. Where might I find a word like it to describe the highest! If I took the purest, most sparkling concept from the inner treasure-chamber of the philosophers, I could only capture thereby an unbinding product of thought. I could not capture the presence of Him whom the generations of men have honoured and degraded with their awesome living and dying. I do indeed mean Him whom the hell-tormented and heaven-storming generations of men mean. Certainly, they draw caricatures and write "God" underneath; they murder one another and say "in God's name." But when all madness and delusion fall to dust, when they stand over against Him in the loneliest darkness and no longer say "He, He" but rather sigh "Thou," shout "Thou," all of them the one word, and when they then add "God," is it not the real God whom they all implore, the One Living God, the God of the children of man? Is it not He who hears them? And just for this reason is not the word "God," the word of appeal, the word which has become a *name,* consecrated in all human tongues for all times? We must esteem those who interdict it because they rebel against the injustice and wrong which are so readily referred to "God" for authorization. But we may not give it up. How understandable it is that some suggest we should remain silent about the "last things" for a time in order that the misused words may be redeemed! But they are not to be redeemed *thus.* We cannot cleanse the word "God" and we cannot make it whole; but, defiled and mutilated as it is, we can raise it from the ground and set it over an hour of great care.

MARTIN BUBER: *Eclipse of God*

This God of the Jews was not a nature God. He was something more. He was the God of nature. He did not in some way symbolize the cycle of nature, dying with the harvest and resurrecting at the time of sowing as did the grain-kings of the fertility religions. He made the harvest and He ordained the passing of the seasons and He ordered the movements of the planets. Nature's Cause and Creator, beyond nature, He "formeth the mountains and createth the wind and declareth unto man what is His thought, that maketh the morning darkness and treadeth on the high places of the earth." He is not part of nature. Nature itself is His domain. "The beasts of the field are Mine. Mine are the cattle upon a thousand hills." He it is who "laid the foundations of the earth . . . when the morning stars praised Me together and all the sons of God made a joyful music." Thus the Jews reached a concept of God which differed in vital respects from any other insight achieved by the ancient world. On the one hand, God was Lord of nature, separate from it and in no way immersed in its fatalities. The Jews had no part in the polytheism of the fertility religions. But since Creation was the work of God's hands, it could not be dismissed as an illusion, as a mere transitory flux of appearances, as the *maya* of Indian philosophers or the recurring and unchanging cycle of Greek thought.

This picture gave a peculiar vitality to the Jewish concept of God and a special value to the Jewish idea of the world and of time. The vitality is quite simply the overwhelming impression of a *living* God. His ways might be unsearchable and His wisdom incomprehensible. He might be as remote from human understanding as the pure Being adored by the Brahmans or the ultimate Rationality sought for by the

Greeks. But He was never in any danger of becoming an abstraction. Father, Creator, Worker, Judge—He floods the holy books of the Jewish people with an enormous, almost an appalling vitality. The Jews themselves felt it. "It is a terrible thing to fall into the hands of the living God." So often we think of "being"—if we think of it at all—as the last anonymous something left when all recognizable qualities have been abstracted. But the God who declared Himself "I am who am" to Moses, represents the fullness of being, its inexhaustible energy (which only in the atomic age can we even faintly grasp), its plenitude of quality, its torrent of life.

BARBARA WARD: *Faith and Freedom*

. . . **the 90th Psalm . . . starts** with a song of praise: "Lord, thou hast been our dwelling place age after age." In order to describe human transitoriness, the poet glorifies the Divine Eternity. Before looking downward he looks upward. Before considering man's misery he points to God's majesty. Only because we look at something infinite can we realize that we are finite. Only because we are able to see the eternal can we see the limited time that is given us. Only because we can elevate ourselves above the animals can we see that we are like animals. Our melancholy about our transitoriness is rooted in our power to look beyond it. Modern pessimists do not start their writings by praising the Eternal God. They think that they can approach man directly and speak about his finiteness, misery and tragedy. But they do not succeed. Hidden—often to themselves—is a criterion by which they measure and condemn human existence. It is something beyond man. When the Greek poets called men the "mortals", they had in mind the immortal gods by which they measured human mortality. The measure of man's transitoriness is God's eternity; the measure of man's misery and tragedy is the Divine Perfection. That is what the psalmist means when he calls God our dwelling place, the only permanence in the change of all the ages and generations. That is why he starts his song of profoundest melancholy with the praise of the Lord.

PAUL TILLICH: *The Shaking of the Foundations*

God, Who stands so decisively over against our life, the Source of all splendour and all joy, is yet in closest and most cherishing contact with us; and draws us, beyond all splendour and joy, into Truth. He has created in us such a craving for Himself alone, that even the brief flashes of Eternity which sometimes visit us make all else seem dust and ashes, lifeless and unreal. Hence there should be no situation in our life, no attitude, no pre-occupation or relationship, from which we cannot look up to this God of absolute Truth and say *"Our Father,"* of ourselves and of all other souls involved. Our inheritance *is* God, our Father and Home. We recognize him, says St. John of the Cross, because we already carry in our hearts a rough sketch of the beloved countenance. Looking into these deeps, as into a quiet pool in the dark forest, we there find looking back at us the Face we implicitly long for and already know. It is set in another world, another light: yet it is here. As we realize this, our prayer widens until it embraces the extremes of awestruck adoration and confident love, and fuses them in one.

EVELYN UNDERHILL: *An Anthology of the Love of God*

[These are] four ways among the many in which the human creature experiences the fact of God and God is disclosed to men. . . .

First, in History we find the Supernatural penetrating Process and revealed through it.

Next, in Incarnation—and, depending from this, in the fact of sanctity—we find the Supernatural penetrating Personality and revealed through it.

Thirdly, in Sacraments and Symbols, we find the Supernatural penetrating created Things, and revealed to the soul through the channels of sense.

Last, in Prayer we find the Supernatural in immediate contact with created spirit; self-revealed within the Individual Soul.

EVELYN UNDERHILL: *An Anthology of the Love of God*

That which we really know about God is not what we have been clever enough to find out, but what the Divine Charity has secretly revealed.

EVELYN UNDERHILL: *An Anthology of the Love of God*

Natural theology, as I understand it, is necessarily a department of Christian theology, a phase of Christian intellectualism. It cannot compose or correspond to a religion because after all it consists of no more than a series of inferences, whereas a real living religion is not a series of inferences but a confrontation with reality. A living religion is something which happens, not when and because man infers (however valid his inferences may be), but when and because God acts and speaks. The great makers and architects of systems of natural theology, Thomas Aquinas, for example, see this clearly enough. For them the culminating point of natural theology is when it demonstrates the need for revelation. It shows the emptiness of a niche which philosophy can perceive but which it cannot fill. From this point of view natural theology has a relationship to the Christian revelation akin to that of the relationship of Hebrew prophecy to the great self-revealing acts of God in the life, death, and Resurrection of Jesus Christ.

J. V. LANGMEAD CASSERLEY: *Graceful Reason*

A God as all-present and all-powerful and all-loving as the one proclaimed by the historic creeds is a God entitled to pick any lock and batter down any door. The fact that the creeds are true is no reason for assuming that God can and will work only through those who believe them to be true. God roams; He breaks; He enters; He is not above using an alias; He chooses and stations His witnesses where He will.

CHAD WALSH: *Behold the Glory*

He is inaccessible yet He is close at hand. He encompasses man on all sides. There is not just one way to God, as there is to an oasis across the desert or to a new mathematical idea across the breadth of the science of number. For man there are as many ways of approach to God as there are wanderings on the earth or paths to his own heart.

JACQUES MARITAIN: *Approaches to God*

It is not sufficient to place yourself daily under God. What really matters is to be *only* under God: the slightest division of allegiance opens the door to daydreaming, petty conversation, petty boasting, petty malice—all the petty satellites of the death-instinct.

"But how, then, am I to love God?" "You must love Him as if He were a non-God, a non-Spirit, a non-Person, a non-Substance: love

Him simply as the One, the pure and absolute Unity in which is no trace of Duality. And into this One, we must let ourselves fall continually from being into non-being. God helps us to do this."

DAG HAMMARSKJÖLD: Markings

How blessed and marvellous are the gifts of God, beloved. Life in immortality, splendor in righteousness, truth in boldness, faith in confidence, discipline in holiness: all these are in our understanding. What, then, are the things prepared for those who endure? The Creator and Father of the Ages, the all-holy one himself knows their number and beauty.

CLEMENT OF ROME (First Century)

We see that God provides all things, and we do not suppose that he stands in need of the material offerings of men. But we are taught, and believe with conviction, that he accepts only those who imitate those virtues of the divine character, such as moderation, righteousness and love of man; such qualities as are the essential properties of God, who has no name ascribed to him: we are taught that he, being good, made all things in the beginning out of formless matter, for the sake of mankind; and if by their deeds men show themselves worthy in respect of his purpose, we believe that they are admitted to his society, to reign with him, released from corruption and suffering. For as he made us at the beginning from non-existence, so we suppose that those who choose what is pleasing to him are, in virtue of that choice, admitted to immortality and fellowship with God. For our original birth was not a matter of our choice; but the pursuit of those objects which he desires us to pursue, exercising choice through the rational powers which he has bestowed on us—to this he persuades us, and leads us to faith.

JUSTIN MARTYR (Second Century)

First then, lest any man in his dejection of spirit, or of fortune, should stray into a jealousie or suspition of Gods power to deliver him, As God hath spangled the firmament with starres, so hath he his Scriptures with names, and Metaphors, and denotations of power. Sometimes he shined out in the name of a *Sword,* and of a *Target,* and of a

Wall, and of a *Tower,* and of a *Rocke,* and of a *Hill;* And sometimes in that glorious and manifold constellation of all together, *Dominus exercitum, The Lord of Hosts.* God, as God, is never represented to us, with Defensive Armes; He needs them not. When the Poets present their great Heroes, and their Worthies, they alwayes insist upon their Armes, they spend much of their invention upon the description of their Armes; both because the greatest valour and strength needs Armes, (*Goliah* himselfe was armed) and because to expose ones selfe to danger unarmed, is not valour, but rashnesse. But God is invulnerable in himselfe, and is never represented armed; you finde no shirts of mayle, no Helmets, no Cuirasses in Gods Armory.

JOHN DONNE: *Sermons*

Our first step then in this first part, is, the *sociablenesse,* the communicablenesse of God; He loves holy meetings, he loves the *communion of Saints,* the *household of the faithfull: Deliciae ejus,* says Solomon, *his delight is to be with the Sons of men,* and that the Sons of men should be with him: Religion is not a *melancholy;* the spirit of God is not a *dampe;* the Church is not a *grave:* it is a *fold,* it is an *Arke,* it is a *net,* it is a *city,* it is *a kingdome,* not only a house, but a house that hath *many mansions* in it: still it is a *plurall* thing, consisting of *many:* and very good *grammarians* amongst the *Hebrews,* have thought, and said that that *name,* by which God notifies himself to the world, in the very beginning of *Genesis,* which is *Elohim,* as it is a *plurall word* there, so it hath no *singular:* they say we cannot name God, but *plurally:* so sociable, so communicable, so extensive, so derivative of himself, is God, and so manifold are the beames, and the emanations that flow out from him.

JOHN DONNE: *Sermons*

Men have addressed their eternal *Thou* with many names. In singing of Him who was thus named they always had the *Thou* in mind: the first myths were hymns of praise. Then the names took refuge in the language of *It;* men were more and more strongly moved to think of and to address their eternal *Thou* as an *It.* But all God's names are hallowed, for in them He is not merely spoken about, but also spoken to.

Many men wish to reject the word God as a legitimate usage, because it is so misused. It is indeed the most heavily laden of all the words used by men. For that very reason it is the most imperishable and most indispensable. What does all mistaken talk about God's being and works (though there has been, and can be, no other talk about these) matter in comparison with the one truth that all men who have addressed God had God Himself in mind? For he who speaks the word God and really has *Thou* in mind (whatever the illusion by which he is held), addresses the true *Thou* of his life, which cannot be limited by another *Thou,* and to which he stands in a relation that gathers up and includes all others.

But when he, too, who abhors the name, and believes himself to be godless, gives his whole being to addressing the *Thou* of his life, as a *Thou* that cannot be limited by another, he addresses God.

MARTIN BUBER: *I and Thou*

Where is the emphasis in the Creed? Is it *"I* believe in God"? Or is it "I believe in *God"?* There is no doubt where the answer of all wholesome religion lies . . . the thing that is important is that there is a God to believe in. There is a story of a young lady who asked Dr. Jowett, "Oh Master, do tell me—what do you think about God?" To which the Master replied, "That, my dear young lady, is a very unimportant question; the only thing that signifies is what He thinks about me." In all our efforts to study religious life, whether in our own or in other forms of faith, and to build up our conscience, our character, even to determine our form of service, if these things once get into the first place, the whole religious life is wrecked; you have got away from the one reality—God, and are centering upon your own feelings and activities. . . . In the New Testament, if it is true at all, we are face to face with God; if that is not true, the New Testament is written under an illusion from end to end. It would be a very interesting illusion, and it would be thoroughly worth while to study it, for it has produced great effects in the history of the world, but an illusion all the same. The men who wrote the books of the New Testament believed that in Jesus Christ, God Himself lived and walked about among them. "The Word was made flesh and dwelt among us." They start from there.

WILLIAM TEMPLE: *The Universality of Christ*

The Eclipse of God

Behold, the days come, saith the Lord God, that I will send a famine in the land, not a famine of bread, nor a thirst for water, but of hearing the words of the Lord:

And they shall wander from sea to sea, and from the north even to the east, they shall run to and fro to seek the word of the Lord, and shall not find it.

AMOS 8:11–12 KJV

Eclipse of the light of heaven, eclipse of God—such indeed is the character of the historic hour through which the world is passing. But it is not a process which can be adequately accounted for by instancing the changes that have taken place in man's spirit. An eclipse of the sun is something that occurs between the sun and our eyes, not in the sun itself. Nor does philosophy consider us blind to God. Philosophy holds that we lack to-day only the spiritual orientation which can make possible a reappearance "of God and the gods," a new procession of sublime images. But when, as in this instance, something is taking place between heaven and earth, one misses everything when one insists on discovering within earthly thought the power that unveils the mystery. He who refuses to submit himself to the effective reality of the transcendence as such—our vis-à-vis—contributes to the human responsibility for the eclipse.

MARTIN BUBER: Eclipse of God

Sartre accepts Nietzsche's cry, or better shout, "God is dead!" as a valid statement of fact. Our generation appears to him as specifically the one which has outlived God. He says once—although elsewhere he most emphatically asserts, as one who knows, *"Dieu n'existe pas"*—that the fact that God is dead does not mean that he does not exist nor even that he no longer exists. In place of these interpretations he presents another which is singular enough. "He is dead," he says, "he spoke to us and now is silent, all that we touch now is his corpse." I shall not deal here with the shockingly trivial concluding sentence. But let us turn to that which precedes it: "He spoke to us and now he is silent." Let us try to take it seriously, that is, let us ignore what Sartre really meant by it, namely, that man in earlier times believed that he heard

God and now is no longer capable of so believing. Let us ask whether it may not be literally true that God formerly spoke to us and is now silent, and whether this is not to be understood as the Hebrew Bible understands it, namely, that the living God is not only a self-revealing but also a self-concealing God. Let us realize what it means to live in the age of such a concealment, such a divine silence, and we shall perhaps understand its implication for our existence as something entirely different from that which Sartre desires to teach us. . . .

God can never become an object for me; I can attain no other relation to Him than that of the I to its eternal Thou, that of the Thou to its eternal I. But if man is no longer able to attain this relation, if God is silent toward him and he toward God, then something has taken place, not in human subjectivity but in Being itself. It would be worthier not to explain it to oneself in sensational and incompetent sayings, such as that of the "death" of God, but to endure it as it is and at the same time to move existentially toward a new happening, toward that event in which the word between heaven and earth will again be heard. Thus the perseverance of the "religious need," to which Sartre objects and which he thinks contradicts the silence of the transcendent, instead points directly to the situation in which man becomes aware of this silence as such.

MARTIN BUBER: *Eclipse of God*

God does not die on the day when we cease to believe in a personal deity, but we die on the day when our lives cease to be illumined by the steady radiance, renewed daily, of a wonder, the source of which is beyond all reason.

DAG HAMMARSKJÖLD: *Markings*

The wisdom of this world in all its forms cannot know God, and the power of this world with all its means cannot reach God. If they try it, they produce idolatry and are revealed in their foolishness which is the foolishness of idolatry.

PAUL TILLICH: *The New Being*

It does not rest with the soul to believe in the reality of God if God does not reveal this reality. In trying to do so it either labels something else with the name of God, and that is idolatry, or else its belief in God remains abstract and verbal. Such a belief prevails wherever religious dogma is taken for granted, as is the case with those centuries and countries in which it never enters anyones's head to question it. The state of nonbelief is then what Saint John of the Cross calls a night. The belief is verbal and does not penetrate the soul. At a time like the present, incredulity may be equivalent to the dark night of Saint John of the Cross if the unbeliever loves God, if he is like the child who does not know whether there is bread anywhere, but who cries out because he is hungry.

SIMONE WEIL: *Waiting for God*

For there *is* a God, and He's here, immediate, accessible. I don't hold with those thinkers that believe in this time He is farther away—that in the Middle Ages, for instance, He was closer. He is equally accessible now, not only in works of art or in the glories of a particular religious service, or in the light, the aftermath that follows the dark night of the soul, but in the lowest forms of life, He moves and has His being. Nobody has killed off the snails. Is this a new thought? Hardly. But it needs some practicing in Western society.

THEODORE ROETHKE: "On 'Identity,' "
in *On the Poet and His Craft*

The Fear of God

All religious reality begins with what Biblical religion calls the "fear of God." It comes when our existence between birth and death becomes incomprehensible and uncanny, when all security is shattered through the mystery. This is not the relative mystery of that which is inaccessible only to the present state of human knowledge and is hence in principle discoverable. It is the essential mystery, the inscrutableness of which belongs to its very nature; it is the unknowable. Through this dark gate (which is only a gate and not, as some theologians believe, a dwelling) the believing man steps forth into the everyday which is henceforth hallowed as the place in which he has to live with the mystery. He steps forth directed and assigned to the concrete, contextual situations of his existence. That he henceforth accepts the situation as given him by the Giver is what Biblical religion calls the "fear of God."

An important philosopher of our day, Whitehead, asks how the Old Testament saying that the fear of God is the beginning of wisdom is to be reconciled with the New Testament saying that God is love. Whitehead has not fully grasped the meaning of the word "beginning." He who begins with the love of God without having previously experienced the fear of God, loves an idol which he himself has made, a god whom it is easy enough to love. He does not love the real God who is, to begin with, dreadful and incomprehensible. Consequently, if he then perceives, as Job and Ivan Karamazov perceive, that God is dreadful and incomprehensible, he is terrified. He despairs of God and of the world if God does not take pity on him, as He did on Job, and bring him to love Him Himself.

MARTIN BUBER: *Eclipse of God*

Forgetting that there exists such a state as salutary dread, modern man has become spiritually foolhardy. His bravado, I suspect, will stand the test no better than ancient Pistol's. He who admits no fear of God is really a post-Christian man; for at the heart of Judaism and Christianity lies a holy dread. And a good many people, outwardly and perhaps inwardly religious—for *religio* implies the cult, the common worship, the binding together, rather than the relationship between the Almighty and lonely man—today deny the reality of reverential fear, and thus are post-Christian without confessing it.

RUSSELL KIRK: "The Rarity of the God-Fearing Man," in *The Intemperate Professor*

Mere enlightened self-interest will submit to any strong evil. In one aspect or another, fear insists upon forcing itself into our lives. If the fear of God is obscured, then obsessive fear of suffering, poverty, and sickness will come to the front; or if a well-cushioned state keeps most of these worries at bay, then the tormenting neuroses of modern man, under the labels of "insecurity" and "anxiety" and "constitutional inferiority," will be the dominant mode of fear. And these latter forms of fear are the more dismaying, for there are disciplines by which one may diminish one's fear of God. But to remedy the causes of fear from the troubles of our time is beyond the power of the ordinary individual; and to put the neuroses to sleep, supposing any belief in a transcendent order to be absent, there is only the chilly comfort of the analyst's couch or the tranquillizing drug.

RUSSELL KIRK: "The Rarity of the God-
Fearing Man," in The Intemperate Professor

Since it is commonly agreed that if our life is without religion we are most miserable and in no way better than brute animals, no one wishes to be considered as completely alienated from piety and acknowledgement of God. There is, however, a great difference in the way of declaring one's religion, because the majority of men are not truly touched by the awe of God. Yet, willingly, or not, they are bound by this thought always coming anew to their minds that there is some divinity by whose power they stand or fall. Hence, being astonished by the thought of such a great power, they revere it in some way in order not to provoke it against themselves by too great a contempt. Yet, living in a disorderly way and rejecting all honesty, they exhibit a great sense of security in despising the judgment of God. Moreover, they turn away from the true God because they estimate God not by his infinite majesty but by the foolish and giddy vanity of their own mind. Hence, although they may afterward strive to serve God with great care, that does not profit them at all, because they do not worship the eternal God, but the dreams and fancies of their own heart in place of God. Now the gist of true piety does not consist in a fear which would gladly flee the judgment of God but, being unable to do so, has horror of it. True piety consists rather in a pure and true zeal which loves God altogether as Father, and reveres him truly as Lord, embraces his justice and dreads to offend him more than to die. All those who possess this zeal do not undertake to forge for themselves a God as their temerity wishes, but they seek the knowledge of the true God from that very God and do not conceive him otherwise than he manifests and declares himself to them.

JOHN CALVIN: Instruction in Faith

It is safe to say that a man who has never tried to flee God has never experienced the God Who is really God. . . . The pious man of the Old Testament, the mystical saint of the Middle Ages, the reformer of the Christian Church, and the prophet of atheism are all united through that tremendous human experience: man cannot stand the God Who is really God. Man tries to escape God, and hates Him, because he cannot escape Him. The protest against God, the will that there be no God, and the flight to atheism are all genuine elements of profound religion. And only on the basis of these elements has religion meaning and power.

PAUL TILLICH: *The Shaking of the Foundations*

... the conditions of modern industrial civilization do not strongly encourage the search after God. To the average Western man today, the good things of life appear to come almost automatically, out of factories and department stores; they seem to be man's creations and his birthright. The old-fashioned farmer knew he was dependent on God's providence; twentieth-century urban man looks to the government, the corporation, and the giant union for protection and plenty. The Protestant of yesteryear passionately sought the salvation of his soul, endeavoring to establish a personal relationship with divine mercy. The average American, some Protestants told me, now tends to tolerate God, rather than to fear Him. As one young coed remarked, "Yes, I believe in God, but I'm not nuts about Him."

RUSSELL KIRK: "The Impenitent Religionist,"
in *The Intemperate Professor*

Every age portrays God in the image of its poetry and its politics. In one century, God is an absolute monarch, exacting his due; in another century, still an absolute sovereign, but a benevolent despot; again, perhaps a grand gentleman among aristocrats; at a different time, a democratic president, with an eye to the ballot box. It has been said that to many of our generation, God is a Republican and works in a bank; but this image is giving way, I think, to God as Chum—at worst, God as a playground supervisor. So much for the images. But in reality God does not alter.

Because the graven image deludes, it is forbidden. Yet a mental image of some sort men demand, in any time. . . . The deceptive image, formed by our petty preferences in taste or politics, may do remarkable mischief. And God the Chum, never to be dreaded because He is indiscriminately affectionate—even promiscuous—may be a more treacherous idol, and more potent for the destruction of personality and of the civil social order, than the vision of God that had Agag hewed in pieces.

RUSSELL KIRK: "The Rarity of the God-Fearing Man," in *The Intemperate Professor*

Death is the work of the Divine wrath: "For all our days are passed away in thy wrath, we bring our years to an end as a sigh"—as short as a sigh, and as full of sorrow as a sigh. The idea of the Divine wrath has become strange to our time. We have rejected a religion which seemed to make God a furious tyrant, an individual with passions and desires who committed arbitrary acts. This is not what the wrath of God means. It means the inescapable and unavoidable reaction against every distortion of the law of life, and above all against human pride and arrogance. That reaction, through which man is thrown back into his limits, is not a passionate act of punishment or vengeance on the part of God. It is the reestablishment of the balance between God and man, which is disturbed by man's elevation against God.

PAUL TILLICH: *The Shaking of the Foundations*

Our age, having dispensed almost entirely with fear of God, now finds itself paralyzed with dread when it contemplates man and his powers; and what makes this dread so acute is precisely the loss of faith —the sense that modern civilization has gone empty at the core.

DAVID E. ROBERTS: *The Grandeur and Misery of Man*

The Person of Christ

Christ be with me, Christ within me,
    Christ behind me, Christ before me,
Christ beside me, Christ to win me,
    Christ to comfort and restore me,
Christ beneath me, Christ above me,
    Christ in quiet, Christ in danger,
Christ in hearts of all that love me,
    Christ in mouth of friend and stranger.

ST. PATRICK

What does the Church think of Christ? The Church's answer is categorical and uncompromising, and it is this: That Jesus Bar-Joseph, the carpenter of Nazareth, was in fact and in truth, and in the most exact and literal sense of the words, the God "by whom all things were made." His body and brain were those of a common man; His personality was the personality of God, so far as that personality could be expressed in human terms. He was not a kind of demon or fairy pretending to be human; He was in every respect a genuine living man. He was not merely a man so good as to be "like God"—He *was* God.

Now this is not just a pious commonplace; it is not commonplace at all. For what it means is this, among other things; that for whatever reason God chose to make man as he is—limited and suffering and subject to sorrows and death—He had the honesty and the courage to take His own medicine. Whatever game He is playing with His creation, He has kept His own rules and played fair. He can exact nothing from man that He has not exacted from Himself. He has Himself gone through the whole of human experience, from the trivial irritations of family life and the cramping restrictions of hard work and lack of money to the worst horrors of pain and humiliation, defeat, despair, and death. When He was a man, He played the man. He was born in poverty and died in disgrace and thought it well worth while.

DOROTHY L. SAYERS: Creed or Chaos

The Christ event which Christian faith regards, retrospectively, as the culmination of history could not be regarded prospectively as such a fulfillment. It is however the more impressive retrospectively because it could not be fully anticipated. It is the more impressive because some of the expectations hoped for the fulfillment and vindication of forces and factors in history (the nation and the "righteous") which do not deserve to be singled out as the bearers of historic fulfillment. The Christ was expected to be a triumphant Messiah, and he is in fact a "suffering servant" who does not bring the struggle between good and evil to a triumphant conclusion. Instead, the drama of his life reveals that the nominally "righteous" are involved in the crucifixion and that the only resolution of the variance between God and man was for God to take the sins of men upon Himself. Thus the suffering Messiah became, in the eyes of faith, a clue to the mystery of the mercy and the justice of God, and the atonement became the real content of the revelation. On these grounds the Christ event was recognized to be the "end" of history, not in the sense of its "finis" but as its *telos*. History would go on, and human pride and arrogance would create unimaginable evils. But nothing would surprise or dismay the person who had once penetrated to the mystery by the help of this key.

REINHOLD NIEBUHR: *The Self and the Dramas of History*

Let us, in Heaven's name, drag out the Divine Drama from under the dreadful accumulation of slipshod thinking and trashy sentiment heaped upon it, and set it on an open stage to startle the world into some sort of vigorous reaction. If the pious are the first to be shocked, so much the worse for the pious—others will pass into the Kingdom of Heaven before them. If all men are offended because of Christ, let them be offended; but where is the sense of their being offended at something that is not Christ and is nothing like Him? We do Him singularly little honor by watering down His personality till it could not offend a fly. Surely it is not the business of the Church to adapt Christ to men, but to adapt men to Christ.

It is the dogma that is the drama—not beautiful phrases, nor comforting sentiments, nor vague aspirations to loving-kindness and uplift, nor the promise of something nice after death—but the terrifying assertion that the same God who made the world lived in the world and passed through the grave and gate of death. Show that to the heathen, and they may not believe it; but at least they may realize that here is something that a man might be glad to believe.

DOROTHY L. SAYERS: *Creed or Chaos*

(On the story of the Gadarene swine, Luke 8.)
. . . "What have you to do with me, Jesus, Son of the Most High God? I beseech you, do not torment me."

If you want to miss the point of the story entirely, then dismiss this outcry as the ravings of a demented man with whom you have nothing in common. Embrace the happy fiction that most human beings delight to bask in the presence of perfect Goodness. The only trouble is that you then find the resistance to Christianity down through the centuries quite unaccountable.

The plain fact is that Christ is a kind of plague to the human race. There is something in all of us that cries out at times: "What a relief it would be if I could just go ahead and live without having that Figure rise before my vision! Why can't he leave me alone?" We are tormented partly because His presence makes us fully aware of our misery and bondage, and partly because it threatens to take away from us those ills and obsessions that we cling to because they seem to be our very selves.

DAVID E. ROBERTS: *The Grandeur and Misery of Man*

The mystery of Reality enters history very gently by a human channel and shows the character of Perfect Love within the life of man; gives us something to hold on to, a Truth which is also a Way and a Life. What we see is not very sensational: but if we look at it steadily, it pierces the heart. First we see a baby and a long, hidden growth; and then the unmeasured outpouring and self-spending of an other-worldly love and mercy, teaching, healing, rescuing, transforming, but never trying to get anything for itself. And when we look deeper, we see beyond this a mysterious self-imparting and a more mysterious anguish and struggle; consummated at last in the most generous and lonely of deaths, issuing in a victory which has given life ever since to men's souls. Through this vivid life—what Christ does and how He does it, His prayer, His compassionate healing action, His use of suffering, His communion with God and man—the light of Reality floods our twilit inner lives; showing us the human transfigured by the Divine. This is what St. Ignatius Loyola intended and desired when he taught his pupils to "contemplate the Mysteries of the Life of Christ."

Few people do it properly. They are too anxious to get on and be practical: for the lesson of the one thing needful is a lesson which human nature instinctively resists. Yet we shall make our own small work of art all the better if we soak our souls in that beauty first.

EVELYN UNDERHILL: *An Anthology of the Love of God*

The world is not saved by evolution but by incarnation. The more deeply we enter into prayer the more certain we become of this. Nothing can redeem the lower and bring back to health, but a life-giving incursion from the higher; a manifestation of the already present Reality. "I came forth from the Father and am come into the world": and this perpetual advent—the response of the eternal Agape to Eros in his need—is the true coming into time of the Kingdom of Heaven. The Pentecostal energy and splendour is present to glorify every living thing: and sometimes our Love reaches the Level at which it sees this as a present fact and the actual is transfigured by the real.

What we look for, then, is not Utopia, but something which is given from beyond: Emmanuel, God with us, the whole creation won from rebellion and consecrated to the creative purposes of Christ. This means something far more drastic than the triumph of international justice and good social conditions. It means the transfiguration of the natural order by the supernatural: by the Eternal Charity. Though we achieve social justice, liberty, peace itself, though we give our bodies to be burned for these admirable causes, if we lack charity we are nothing. For the Kingdom is the Holy, not the moral; the Beautiful, not the correct; the Perfect, not the adequate; Charity, not law.

EVELYN UNDERHILL: *An Anthology of the Love of God*

The powers exercised by Christ constituted, not a proof, but a link in the chain of a demonstration. They were the certain sign that Christ was placed outside the ordinary run of humanity, among those who have given themselves either to evil or to good. They didn't indicate which. But it was easy to see which it was by the manifest perfection of Christ, the purity of his life, the perfect beauty of his words, and the fact that he only exercised his powers in order to perform acts of compassion. All this was merely the proof that he was a saint. But those who were certain he was a saint, when they listened to him declaring himself to be the Son of God, might hesitate as to the precise meaning of these words, but were bound to believe that they contained a truth. For when a saint says such things, he cannot either be lying or mistaken. We, in the same way, are bound to believe all that Christ has said, save where we have the right to suppose a faulty transcription, and what gives the proof its force is beauty. When the subject in question is the good, beauty is a rigorous and positive proof; and, indeed, there can be none other. It is absolutely impossible for there to be any other.

Christ said, "If I had not done among them the works which none other man did, they had not had sin"; but he also said, "If I had not come and spoken unto them, they had not had sin" [John 15:24 and 22]. Elsewhere he speaks about his "mighty works" [Matthew 11:21]. Acts and words are classed together. The exceptional character of the acts had no other object than to draw attention. Once the attention had been drawn, there can be no other form of proof than beauty, purity, perfection.

The words addressed to Thomas, "Blessed are they that have not seen, and yet have believed" [John 20:29], cannot refer to those who, without having seen it, believe in the fact of the resurrection. That would be praising credulity, not faith. There are old women everywhere who are only too ready to believe no matter what tale about dead people returned to life. Surely those who are called blessed are they who have no need of the resurrection in order to believe, and for whom Christ's perfection and the Cross are in themselves proof.

Thus from the religious point of view the miracles are of secondary importance, and from the scientific point of view they enter naturally into the scientific conception of the world. As for the idea of proving God's existence by a violation of the laws of nature, it would doubtless have appeared to the early Christians as monstrous. It could only arise in our diseased minds, which think that the fixed order of the world is able to offer legitimate arguments to atheists.

SIMONE WEIL: *The Need for Roots*

The miracles of Jesus were the ordinary works of His Father, wrought small and swift that we might take them in. . . . In all His miracles He did only in miniature what His Father does ever in the great. Poor, indeed, was the making of the wine in the . . . pots of stone, compared with its making in the lovely growth of the vine with its clusters of swelling grapes—the live roots gathering from the earth the water that had to be borne in pitchers and poured into the great vases; but it is precious as the interpreter of the same, even in its being the outcome of Our Lord's sympathy with ordinary human rejoicing.

GEORGE MACDONALD

In the days of His earthly ministry, only those could speak to Him who came where He was. If He was in Galilee, men could not find Him in Jerusalem; if He was in Jerusalem, men could not find Him in

Galilee. But His Ascension means that He is perfectly united with God; we are with Him wherever we are present to God; and that is everywhere and always. Because He is "in Heaven" He is everywhere on earth; because He is ascended, He is here now. Our devotion is not to hold us by the empty tomb; it must lift up our hearts to heaven so that we too "in heart and mind thither ascend and with Him continually dwell"; it must also send us forth into the world to do His will; and these are not two things, but one.

WILLIAM TEMPLE: *Readings in St. John's Gospel*

I had said of Christ that he ranks with the poets. That is true. But his entire life also is the most wonderful of poems, for "pity and terror" there is nothing in the entire cycle of Greek tragedy to touch it. The absolute purity of the protagonist . . . shows how wrong Aristotle was when he said in his treatise on the drama that it would be impossible to bear the spectacle of the blameless in pain. Not in Aeschylus nor Dante, those stern masters of tenderness, in Shakespeare, the most purely human of all the great artists, in the whole of Celtic myth and legend, where the loveliness of the world is shown through a mist of tears, and the life of a man is no more than the life of a flower, is there anything that, for sheer simplicity of pathos wedded and made one with sublimity of tragic effect, can be said to equal or even approach the last act of Christ's passion. The little supper with his companions, one of whom has already sold him for a price; the anguish in the quiet moon-lit garden; the false friend coming close to him so as to betray him with a kiss; the friend who still believed in him, and on whom as a rock he had hoped to build a house of refuge for Man, denying him as the bird cried to the dawn; his own utter loneliness, his submission, his acceptance of everything; and along with it all such scenes as the high priest of orthodoxy rending his raiment in wrath and the magistrate of civil justice calling for water in the vain hope of cleansing himself of that stain of innocent blood that makes him the scarlet figure of history; the coronation ceremony of sorrow, one of the most wonderful things in the whole of recorded time; the crucifixion of the Innocent One before the eyes of his mother and of the disciples whom he loved; the soldiers gambling and throwing of dice for his clothes, the terrible death by which he gave the world its most eternal symbol; and his final burial in the tomb of the rich man, his body swathed in Egyptian linen with costly spices and perfumes as though he had been a king's son. When one contemplates all this from the point of view of art alone, one cannot but be grateful that the supreme office of the Church should be the playing of the tragedy without the shedding of blood: the mystical presentation, by means of dialogue and costume and gesture even, of the Passion of her Lord; and it is always a source of pleasure and awe to me to remember that the ultimate survival of the Greek chorus, lost elsewhere to art, is to be found in the servitor answering the priest at Mass.

OSCAR WILDE: from *The Tree and the Master,*
ed. by Sister Mary Immaculate

The people who hanged Christ never, to do them justice, accused Him of being a bore—on the contrary; they thought Him too dynamic to be safe. It has been left for later generations to muffle up that shattering personality and surround Him with an atmosphere of tedium. We have very efficiently pared the claws of the Lion of Judah, certified Him "meek and mild," and recommended Him as a fitting household pet for pale curates and pious old ladies. To those who knew Him, however, He in no way suggested a milk-and-water person; *they* objected to Him as a dangerous firebrand. True, He was tender to the unfortunate, patient with honest inquirers, and humble before Heaven; but He insulted respectable clergymen by calling them hypocrites; He referred to King Herod as "that fox"; He went to parties in disreputable company and was looked upon as a "gluttonous man and a wine-bibber, a friend of publicans and sinners"; He assaulted indignant tradesmen and threw them and their belongings out of the Temple; He drove a coach-and-horses through a number of sacrosanct and hoary regulations; He cured diseases by any means that came handy, with a shocking casualness in the matter of other people's pigs and property; He showed no proper deference for wealth or social position; when confronted with neat dialectical traps, He displayed a paradoxical humour that affronted serious-minded people, and He retorted by asking disagreeably searching questions that could not be answered by rule of thumb. He was emphatically not a dull man in His human lifetime, and if He was God, there can be nothing dull about God either.

But He had "a daily beauty in His life that made us ugly," and official-dom felt that the established order of things would be more secure without Him. So they did away with God in the name of peace and quietness.

DOROTHY L. SAYERS: Creed or Chaos

I was by now too experienced in literary criticism to regard the Gospels as myths. They had not the mythical taste. And yet the very matter which they set down in their artless, historical fashion—those narrow, unattractive Jews, too blind to the mythical wealth of the Pagan world around them—was precisely the matter of the great myths. If ever a myth had become fact, had been incarnated, it would be just like this. Myths were like it in one way. Histories were like it in another. But nothing was simply like it. And no person was like the Person it depicted; as real, as recognizable, through all that depth of time, as Plato's Socrates or Boswell's Johnson (ten times more so than Eckermann's Goethe or Lockhart's Scott), yet also numinous, lit by a light from beyond the world, a god. But if a god—we are no longer polytheists—then not a god, but God. Here and here only in all time the myth must become fact; the Word, flesh; God, Man. This is not "a religion," nor "a philosophy." It is the summing up and actuality of them all.

C. S. LEWIS: Surprised by Joy

If He was not a man, who was beaten with blows? And if He were not God, who healed the ear which Peter had cut off, and who restored it to its place?

If He was not a man, whose face was spat upon? And if He were not God, who breathed the Holy Spirit upon the faces of the Apostles?

If He was not a man, who was it stood before Pilate at the judgement seat? And if He were not God, who caused the wife of Pilate to suffer many things in a dream?

If He was not a man, upon whose garments did the soldiers cast lots, dividing them amongst them? And if He were not God, for what reason did the sun grow dark above the Cross?

If He was not a man, who was it hung upon a cross? And if He were not God, who moved the earth from its foundations?

If He was not a man, whose hands were pierced by the nails? And if

He were not God, how was the veil of the temple rent in two, and the rocks split asunder, and the graves opened?

If He was not a man, who cried out, "My God, My God, why hast Thou abandoned me"? And if He were not God, who then hath said, "Father forgive them, for they know not what they do"?

If He was not a man, who hung with thieves upon a cross? And if He were not God, for what cause did He say, "This day thou shalt be with me in paradise"?

If He was not a man, to whom did they offer gall and vinegar? And if He were not God, at whose voice did they shake and tremble?

If He was not a man, whose side was opened by a lance, and then came out blood and water? And if He were not God, who hath broken the gates of hell, and burst the iron bars? And by whose command did the dead that slept in their graves come forth?

If He was not a man, whom did the Apostles behold in the Upper Room? And if He were not God, in what manner did He enter, the doors being closed?

If He was not a man, in whose hand did Thomas feel the wounds of the nails and the lance? And if He was not God to whom did Thomas cry out saying, "My Lord and My God"?

ST. EPHRAEM (306?-373)

If the Lord had not risen living from the tomb; if Mary had not recognized Him in the Garden; if He had not manifested Himself to Cephas; if He had not walked at twilight on a road with two disciples as far as the inn where He heard the sweetest words that humanity has ever addressed to Him, "stay with us, for it is getting towards evening, and the day is now far spent. . . ."; if St. Thomas had not placed his fingers in His wounds which no longer bled; if Christ had not manifested Himself to more than five hundred brethren, the majority of whom were still living when Paul wrote his first Epistle to the Corinthians; and if Paul himself had not been dazzled and thrown to the ground at a turn in the road less by blinding light than by the unendurable sweetness of this name, "I am Jesus, whom thou art persecuting"—if all this history were not history, we would not this morning be an innumerable throng around the empty tomb wherein our hope reposes.

It is precisely because in our eyes there exists no fact more certain and to which more people have borne witness than the Resurrection, that we find it repugnant to look for only a symbol in it, as do those of little faith, in whose eyes things have never transpired as the witnesses have reported.

Nevertheless there is no trait of this life of Christ that is not reflected in ours, miserable as they may be. . . . We are forbidden to be dead persons, we are solemnly enjoined to become living persons again.

FRANÇOIS MAURIAC: *Cain, Where Is Your Brother?*

Seven Stanzas at Easter

Make no mistake: if He rose at all
it was as His body;
if the cells' dissolution did not reverse, the molecules reknit, the amino
    acids rekindle,
the Church will fall.

It was not as the flowers,
each soft Spring recurrent;
it was not as His Spirit in the mouths and fuddled eyes of the eleven
    apostles;
it was as His flesh: ours.

The same hinged thumbs and toes,
the same valved heart
that—pierced—died, withered, paused, and then regathered out of
    enduring Might
new strength to enclose.

Let us not mock God with metaphor,
analogy, sidestepping, transcendence;
making of the event a parable, a sign painted in the faded credulity of
    earlier ages:
let us walk through the door.

The stone is rolled back, not papier-mâché,
not a stone in a story,
but the vast rock of materiality that in the slow grinding of time will
    eclipse for each of us
the wide light of day.

And if we will have an angel at the tomb,
make it a real angel,
weighty with Max Planck's quanta, vivid with hair, opaque in the dawn
  light, robed in real linen
spun on a definite loom.

Let us not seek to make it less monstrous,
for our own convenience, our own sense of beauty,
lest, awakened in one unthinkable hour, we are embarrassed by the
  miracle,
and crushed by remonstrance.

JOHN UPDIKE

In short, the Man Christ Jesus has the decisive place in man's
ageless relationship with God. He is what God means by "Man," He is
what man means by "God."

J. S. WHALE: *Christian Doctrine*

THE CROSS

>What if this present were the world's last night?
>Mark in thy heart, O Soul, where thou dost dwell,
>The picture of Christ crucified, and tell
>Whether that countenance can thee affright;
>Tears in his eyes quench the amazing light,
>Blood fills his frowns, which from his pierced head fell,
>And can that tongue adjudge thee unto hell,
>Which prayed forgiveness for his foes' fierce spite?
>No, no; but as in my idolatry
>I said to all my profane mistresses,
>"Beauty, of pity, foulness only is
>A sign of rigor," so I say to thee,
>"To wicked spirits are horrid shapes assigned,
>This beauteous form assures a piteous mind."

JOHN DONNE

It is perfectly true that the Cross means going beyond the frontiers
of the sensible world and even, in a sense, breaking with it. The final

40   THE IDEA OF GOD

stages of the ascent to which it calls us compel us to cross a threshold, a critical point, where we lose touch with the zone of the realities of the senses. That final "excess," glimpsed and accepted from the first steps, inevitably puts everything we do in a special light and gives it a particular significance. That is exactly where the folly of Christianity lies in the eyes of the "wise" who are not prepared to stake the good which they now hold in their hands on a total "Beyond." But that agonizing flight from the experimental zones—which is what the Cross means—is only (as should be strongly emphasized) the sublime aspect of a law common to *all* life. Towards the summit, wrapped in mist to our human eyes and to which the Cross invites us, we rise by a path which is the way of universal progress. The royal road of the Cross is no more nor less than the road of human endeavour supernaturally righted and prolonged. Once we have fully grasped the meaning of the Cross, we are no longer in danger of finding life sad and ugly. We shall simply have become more attentive to its incomprehensible gravity.

To sum up, Jesus on the Cross is both the symbol and the reality of the immense labour of the centuries which has, little by little, raised up the created spirit and brought it back to the depths of the divine context. He represents (and in a true sense, He is) creation, as, sustained by God, it re-ascends the slopes of being, sometimes clinging to things for support, sometimes tearing itself from them in order to transcend them, and always compensating, by physical suffering, for the setbacks caused by its moral downfalls.

TEILHARD DE CHARDIN: *The Divine Milieu*

In its highest and most general sense, the doctrine of the Cross is that to which all men adhere who believe that the vast movement and agitation of human life opens on to a road which leads somewhere, and that that road *climbs upward.* Life has a term: therefore it imposes a particular direction, orientated, in fact, towards the highest possible spiritualization by means of the greatest possible effort. To admit that group of fundamental principles is already to range oneself among the disciples—of Christ Crucified. Once that first choice has been made, the first distinction has been drawn between the brave who will succeed and the pleasure-seekers who will fail, between the elect and the condemned.

TEILHARD DE CHARDIN: *The Divine Milieu*

Everything reminds us of the cross. We ourselves are made in the form of a cross. Balm and sweetness exhale from the cross. The unction which overflows from the cross inundates our souls in proportion as we unite ourselves with it, holding it tightly against our hearts. The cross contains more wisdom than any book; all who do not know this book are ignorant, however many other books they may have studied. Those only are truly wise who love and consult this book, who study it deeply. Bitter as this book is, they are never happier than when they can immerse themselves in its bitterness. The more they frequent this school, the more they desire to remain there, never do their studies weary them.

ST. JEAN MARIE VIANNEY, CURE OF ARS: from
The Tree and the Master, ed. by Sister Mary Immaculate

From the very beginning the Church has been sure that the series of events which were worked out to their inevitable end in Holy Week sum up and express the deepest secrets of the relation of God to men. That means, of course, that Christianity can never be merely a pleasant or consoling religion. It is a stern business. It is concerned with the salvation through sacrifice and love of a world in which, as we can all see now, evil and cruelty are rampant. Its supreme symbol is the Crucifix—the total and loving self-giving of man to the redeeming purposes of God.

Because we are all the children of God we all have our part to play in His redemptive plan; and the Church consists of those loving souls who have accepted this obligation, with all its costs. Its members are all required to live, each in their own way, through the sufferings and self-abandonment of the Cross; as the only real contribution which they can make to the redemption of the world. Christians, like their Master, must be ready to accept the worst that evil and cruelty can do to them, and vanquish it by the power of love.

For if sacrifice, total self-giving to God's mysterious purpose, is what is asked of us, His answer to that sacrifice is the gift of power. Easter and Whitsuntide complete the Christian Mystery by showing us first our Lord Himself and then His chosen apostles possessed of a new power—the power of the Spirit—which changed every situation in which they were placed. That supernatural power is still the inheritance of every Christian, and our idea of Christianity is distorted and incomplete unless we rely on it. It is this power and only this which can bring in the new Christian society of which we hear so much. We ought to pray for it; expect it, trust it; and as we do this, we shall gradually become more and more sure of it.

EVELYN UNDERHILL: *An Anthology of the Love of God*

What I call the haven, as you know, is the Cross. If it cannot be given me to deserve one day to share the Cross of Christ, at least may I share that of the good thief. Of all the beings other than Christ of whom the Gospel tells us, the good thief is by far the one I most envy. To have been at the side of Christ and in the same state during the crucifixion seems to me a far more enviable privilege than to be at the right hand of his glory.

SIMONE WEIL: *Waiting for God*

As for us men, our misery gives us the infinitely precious privilege of sharing in this distance placed between the Son and his Father. This distance is only separation, however, for those who love. For those who love, separation, although painful, is a good, because it is love. Even the distress of the abandoned Christ is a good. There cannot be a greater good for us on earth than to share in it. God can never be perfectly present to us here below on account of our flesh. But he can be almost perfectly absent from us in extreme affliction. This is the only possibility of perfection for us on earth. That is why the Cross is our only hope. "No forest bears such a tree, with such blossoms, such foliage, and such fruit."

SIMONE WEIL: *Waiting for God*

They took the body down from the Cross and one of the few rich men among the first Christians obtained permission to bury it in a rock tomb in his garden; . . . It was well that the tomb should be sealed with all the secrecy of an ancient eastern sepulchre and guarded by the authority of the Caesars . . . [for] it was the end of a very great thing called human history; the history that was merely human. The mythologies and the philosophies were buried there, the gods and the heroes and the sages. In the great Roman phrase, they had lived. But as they could only live, so they could only die; and they were dead.

On the third day the friends of Christ coming at daybreak to the place found the grave empty and the stone rolled away. In varying ways they realized the new wonder; but even they hardly realized that the world had died in the night. What they were looking at was the first day of a new creation, with a new heaven and a new earth; and in a semblance of the gardener God walked again in the garden, in the cool not of the evening but the dawn.

G. K. CHESTERTON: *The Everlasting Man*

I simply argue that the cross be raised again at the center of the marketplace as well as on the steeple of the church. I am recovering the claim that Jesus was not crucified in a cathedral between two candles, but on a cross between two thieves; on the town garbage heap; at a crossroad so cosmopolitan that they had to write his title in Hebrew and in Latin and in Greek . . . at the kind of place where cynics talk smut, and thieves curse, and soldiers gamble. Because that is where he died. And that is what he died about. And that is where churchmen ought to be, and what churchmen should be about.

GEORGE MACLEOD

REDEMPTION AND GRACE

A Hymn to God the Father

I

Wilt thou forgive that sin where I begun,
   Which is my sin, though it were done before?
Wilt thou forgive those sins, through which I run,
   And do run still: though still I do deplore?
     When thou hast done, thou hast not done,
       For I have more.

II

Wilt thou forgive that sin by which I have won
   Others to sin? and, made my sin their door?
Wilt thou forgive that sin which I did shun
   A year, or two: but wallowed in, a score?
     When thou hast done, thou hast not done,
       For I have more.

III

I have a sin of fear, that when I have spun
My last thread, I shall perish on the shore;
Swear by thy self, that at my death thy Son
Shall shine as he shines now, and heretofore;
And, having done that, Thou hast done,
I fear no more.

JOHN DONNE

We cannot be born anew if the power of the old is not broken within us; and it is not broken so long as it puts the burden of guilt upon us. Therefore religion, prophetic as well as apostolic, pronounced, above all, forgiveness. Forgiveness means that the old is thrown into the past because the new has come. "Remember not" in the prophetic words does not mean to forget easily. If it meant that, forgiveness would not be necessary. Forgiveness means a throwing out of the old, as remembered *and* real at the same time, by the strength of the new which could never be the saving new if it did not carry with it the authority of forgiveness.

PAUL TILLICH: *The Shaking of the Foundations*

Mercy is that by which we are pardoned, even all the falls, faults, failings and weaknesses, that attend us, and that we are incident to, in this our day of temptation: and for this mercy we should pray, and say, "Our Father, forgive us our trespasses." For though mercy is free in the exercise of it to usward, yet God will have us ask, that we may have; as he also saith in the text, "Let us come boldly unto the throne of grace, that we may obtain mercy." That is what David means when he says, "Surely goodness and mercy shall follow me all the days of my life, and I will dwell in the house of the Lord for ever."

And again, "When I say my foot slippeth; thy mercy, O Lord, held me up."

This then is the conclusion, that as there is mercy to be obtained by us at the throne of grace, for the pardon of all our weaknesses, so there is also grace there to be found that will yet strengthen us more, to all good walking and living before him.

JOHN BUNYAN: *The Saint's Privilege and Profit*

Having found in many books different methods of going to God and divers practices of the spiritual life, I thought this would serve rather to puzzle me, than facilitate what I sought after, which was nothing but how to become wholly God's . . . I renounced for the love of Him everything that was not He; and I began to live as though there was none but He and I in the world . . . I worshipped Him the oftenest that I could, keeping my mind in His holy Presence, and recalling it as often as I found it wandered from Him. I found no small pain in this exercise, and yet I continued it notwithstanding all the difficulties that occurred . . . or disquieting myself . . . . I made this my business, as much all the day long as at the appointed times of prayer . . . and though I have done it very imperfectly, yet have I found great advantages by it. . . . When we are faithful to keep ourselves in His holy Presence, and set Him always before us; this not only hinders our offending Him . . . at least wilfully, but it also begets holy freedom, and if I may so speak, a familiarity with God wherewith we ask . . . the graces we stand in need of.

BROTHER LAWRENCE: *The Practice of the Presence of God*

For other people, grace indicates the gifts that one has received from nature or society, and the power to do good things with the help of those gifts. But grace is more than gifts. In grace something is overcome; grace occurs "in spite of" something; grace occurs in spite of separation and estrangement. Grace is the *re*union of life with life, the *re*conciliation of the self with itself. Grace is the acceptance of that which is rejected. Grace transforms fate into a meaningful destiny; it changes guilt into confidence and courage. There is something triumphant in the word "grace": in spite of the abounding of sin grace abounds much more.

PAUL TILLICH: *The Shaking of the Foundations*

The gravest risk confronting the converted man is that he shall hug his new-found salvation to his breast, for fear of putting it in jeopardy. All of us have known people who, having solved some agonizing problem through religion, become afraid to test or risk what has brought them such beatitude. We can understand how they feel, and yet the attitude of Jesus is plain. Real salvation does not so bind us to Him that henceforth we can never take a step without his support. If it is genuine, we shall carry it with us out into the world's temptations and buffetings.

DAVID E. ROBERTS: *The Grandeur and Misery of Man*

Man was so limited: he hadn't even the ingenuity to invent a new vice, the animals knew as much. It was for this world that Christ died: the more evil you saw and heard about you, the greater glory lay around the death: it was too easy to die for what was good or beautiful, for home or a civilization—it needed a God to die for the half-hearted and the corrupt.

GRAHAM GREENE: *The Labyrinthine Ways*

All the parables about the seed are connected with this notion of an impersonal Providence. Grace descends from God upon all beings; what becomes of it depends on what they are; there where it really penetrates, the fruit it bears is the result of a process similar to a mechanical one, and which, like a mechanical one, takes place in a time continuum. The virtue of patience, or to translate the Greek word more accurately, of immobile expectancy, is relative to this necessity of duration.

The nonintervention of God in the operation of grace is expressed as clearly as it possibly can be. "So is the kingdom of God, as if a man should cast seed into the ground; and should sleep, and rise night and day, and the seed should spring and grow up, he knoweth not how. For the earth bringeth forth fruit herself; first the blade, then the ear, after that the full corn in the ear" (Mark 4:26–28).

SIMONE WEIL: *The Need for Roots*

Who but my selfe can conceive the sweetnesse of that salutation, when the Spirit of God says to me in a morning, Go forth to day and preach, and preach consolation, preach peace, preach mercy, And spare my people, spare that people whom I have redeemed with my precious Blood, and be not angry with them for ever; Do not wound them, doe not grinde them, do not astonish them with the bitternesse, with the heavinesse, with the sharpnesse, with the consternation of my judgments. *David* proposes to himself, that he would *Sing of Mercy,* *and of judgement* (Psalm 101:1); but it is of mercy first; and not of judgment at all, otherwise then it will come into a song, as joy and consolation is compatible with it. It hath falne into disputation, and admitted argument, whether ever God inflicted punishments by his good Angels; But that the good Angels, the ministeriall Angels of the Church, are properly his instruments, for conveying mercy, peace, consolation, never fell into question, never admitted opposition. . . .

JOHN DONNE: *Sermons*

Is it not the case that the saving powers are always the ones that we have tried to shut out? Whenever the light dawns, whenever a fresh access of hope lifts a man out of his sin and misery, whenever God's love breaks through and makes him a new creature—it always comes as something he has shut out. He has been willfully blind to it; he has allowed it to dry up inside; he has pressed it down, driven it out of mind, run away from it, disguised it, repudiated it, and tried to forget it. And when that man is rescued, despite himself, it is because, although he has made no place for Christ in his heart, Christ has been born in him just the same. Like the birth of a new child into the world, the birth of the new man takes place in a way which we cannot prevent.

DAVID E. ROBERTS: *The Grandeur and Misery of Man*

The
Idea
of Man

Lord, what is man? Why should he cost Thee
So dear? what had his ruin lost Thee?
Lord, what is man, that Thou hast over-bought
So much a thing of naught?

RICHARD CRASHAW

Why did God create only one Adam and not many at a time?

He did this to demonstrate that one man in himself is an entire universe. Also He wished to teach mankind that he who kills one human being is as guilty as if he had destroyed the entire world. Similarly, he who saves the life of one single human being is as worthy as if he had saved all of humanity.

God created only one man so that people should not try to feel superior to one another and boast of their lineage in this wise: "I am descended from a more distinguished Adam than you."

He also did this so that the heathen should not be able to say that since many men had been created at the same time, it was conclusive proof that there was more than one God.

Lastly, He did this in order to establish His own power and glory. When a maker of coins does his work he uses only one mould and all the coins emerge alike. But the King of Kings, blessed be His name, has created all mankind in the mould of Adam, and even so no man is identical to another. For this reason each person must respect himself and say with dignity:

"God created the world on my account. Therefore let me not lose eternal life because of some vain passion!"

Adapted from the *Agada* in the Talmud:
in *A Treasury of Jewish Folklore,*
ed. by Nathan Ausubel

A young and intelligent priest remarked to me the other day that he thought one of the greatest sources of strength in Christianity today lay in the profoundly pessimistic view it took of human nature. There is a great deal in what he says. The people who are most discouraged and made despondent by the barbarity and stupidity of human behaviour at this time are those who think highly of *Homo Sapiens* as a product of evolution, and who still cling to an optimistic belief in the civilizing influence of progress and enlightenment. To them, the appalling outburst of bestial ferocity in the Totalitarian States, and the obstinate selfishness and stupid greed of Capitalist Society, are not merely shocking and alarming. For them, these things are the utter negation of everything in which they have believed. It is as though the bottom had dropped out of their universe. The whole thing looks like a denial of all reason, and they feel as if they and the world had gone mad together. Now for the Christian, this is not so. He is as deeply shocked and grieved as anybody else, but he is not astonished. He has never thought very highly of human nature left to itself. He has been accustomed to the idea that there is a deep interior dislocation in the very center of human personality, and that you can never, as they say, "make people good by Act of Parliament," just because laws are man-made and therefore partake of the imperfect and self-contradictory nature of man. Humanly speaking, it is not true at all that "truly to know the good is to do the good"; it is far truer to say with St. Paul that "the evil that I would not, that I do"; so that the mere increase of knowledge is of very little help in the struggle to outlaw evil. The delusion of the mechanical perfectibility of mankind through a combined process of scientific knowledge and unconscious evolution has been responsible for a great deal of heartbreak. It is, at bottom, far more pessimistic than Christian pessimism, because, if science and progress break down, there is nothing to fall back upon. Humanism is self-contained—it provides for man no resources outside himself. The Christian dogma of the double nature in man—which asserts that man is disintegrated and necessarily imperfect in himself and all his works, yet closely related by a real unity of substance with an eternal perfection within and beyond him—makes the present parlous state of human society seem both less hopeless and less irrational.

DOROTHY L. SAYERS: *Creed or Chaos*

Christianity is strange. It bids man recognize that he is vile, even abominable; and bids him desire to be like God. Without such a counterpoise, this dignity would make him horribly vain, or this humiliation would make him terribly abject.

BLAISE PASCAL: *Pensées*

The Christian view of what a person is is both proud and humble. This Christian view can best be stated by using an old Jewish story. A certain rabbi used to say that all men should keep in their pockets two pieces of paper, one piece in each pocket. When a man was feeling complacent and self-satisfied, he should take out the piece of paper on which was to be written, "I am dust and ashes." But when he was dejected and dispirited he should take out the other, and on that was to be written, "For my sake was the world created."

I am made from the dust, but it is in God's image that I am made. I am God's creature, one of two thousand millions living upon the earth, yet even the hairs of my head are numbered.

ALAN PATON: "The Person in Community,"
The Christian Idea of Education

Now if you are interested in contradictions, I suggest that you ponder this one. Man is so much at the mercy of temporary ignorance, mass social forces, and his own endocrine glands that he is primarily the *victim* of evil rather than the *doer* of it. And yet man—this *same* man—is thought to be capable of so directing his resources that eventually he will construct a just and stable civilization, if only he can learn how to trust himself instead of relying on God.

Is it any wonder that contemporary Christian thought has sometimes been driven into excess as it tries to put a stick of dynamite under this mountain of wishful thinking? Yet instead of excess, what is really called for is counterpoise. I see no reason why the Church should not make common cause with all scientists, artists, and humanitarians who are struggling for justice and freedom, so long as it retains clarity about its own conception of human nature. For then it will always know that the responsibility whereby man may contribute to his own salvation is inseparable from the responsibility whereby man is the author of his own follies. It is the modern view which splits man apart into an innocent automaton and a potential "godlet." It is the Christian view which sees man as a unity—a responsible, sinful, child of God. From the latter standpoint it is impossible to become blind to man's vileness without at the same time becoming blind to his grandeur.

DAVID E. ROBERTS: *The Grandeur and Misery of Man*

The problem of man is not that God does not speak to him: God *does* speak to everyone who has a human countenance. For this is what makes him man. He who is not able to perceive something ultimate, something infinitely significant, is not a man. Man is man because he is able to receive a word from the dimension of the eternal. The question is not that mankind has not received any word from the Lord; the question is that it has been received and resisted and distorted. This is the predicament of all of us. Human existence is never without that which breaks vertically into it. Man is never without a manifestation of that which is ultimately serious and infinitely meaningful. He is never without a word from the Lord and he never ceases resisting and distorting it, both when he has to hear it and when he has to say it.

PAUL TILLICH: *The New Being*

The misery of man lies in the fragmentary character of his life and knowledge; the greatness of man lies in his ability to know that his being is fragmentary and enigmatic.

PAUL TILLICH: *The Shaking of the Foundations*

The whole man is mortal and immortal at the same time: the whole man is temporal and eternal at the same time; the whole man is judged and saved at the same time, because the Eternal took part in flesh and blood and fear of death.

PAUL TILLICH: *The Shaking of the Foundations*

This is the sense of reading old books and rethinking old thoughts, of the study of history and literature and all the rest of it—it is that we may see man as he is, single and whole, reasoning and choosing and believing, half of this world and half of some other, the only animal who must decide what kind of animal he will be, the only beast it is shameful to call a beast, whose soul, as Boethius said, "albeit in a cloudy memory, yet seeks back his own good, but like a drunken man knows not the way home." God is the teacher; and part of His purpose is that we shall learn that manhood has got to be chosen, that it is not simply the sum of the things that happen to us or the things we buy but it is a story which we write by our own choice.

STEPHEN F. BAYNE, JR.: "God is the Teacher,"
The Christian Idea of Education

Man's State of Being

The proper question to be asked about any creed is not, "Is it pleasant?", but, "Is it true?" "Christianity has compelled the mind of man not because it is the most cheering view of man's existence but because it is truest to the facts." It is unpleasant to be called sinners, and much nicer to think that we all have hearts of gold—but have we? It is agreeable to suppose that the more scientific knowledge we acquire the happier we shall be—but does it look like it? It is encouraging to feel that progress is making us automatically every day and in every way better, and better, and better—but does history support that view? "We hold these truths to be self-evident: that all men were created equal"— but does the external evidence support this *a priori* assertion? Or does experience rather suggest that man is "very far gone from original righteousness and is of his own nature inclined to evil"?

DOROTHY L. SAYERS: *The Mind of the Maker*

The world is a Sea in many respects and assimilations. It is a Sea, as it is bottomlesse to any line, which we can sound it with, and end-lesse to any discovery that we can make of it. The purposes of the world, the wayes of the world, exceed our consideration; But yet we are sure the Sea hath a bottome, and sure that it hath limits, that it cannot overpasse; The power of the greatest in the world, the life of the happiest in the world, cannot exceed those bounds, which God hath placed for them; So the world is a Sea. It is a Sea, as it hath ebbs and floods and no man knowes the true reason of those floods and those ebbs. All men have changes and vicissitudes in their bodies, (they fall sick) And in their estates, (they grow poore) And in their minds, (they become sad) at which changes, (sicknesse, poverty, sadnesse) themselves wonder, and the cause is wrapped up in the purpose and judgement of God onely, and hid even from them that have them; and so the world is a Sea. It is a Sea, as the Sea affords water enough for all the world to drinke, but such water as will not quench the thirst. The world affords conveniences enow to satisfie Nature, but these encrease our thirst with drinking, and our desire growes and enlarges it selfe with our abundance, and though we sayle in a full Sea, yet we lacke water; So the world is a Sea. It is a Sea if we consider the Inhabitants. In the Sea, the greater fish devoure the lesse; and so doe the men of this world too. And as fish, when they mud themselves, have no hands to make themselves cleane, but the current of the waters must worke that; So have the men of this world no means to cleanse themselves from those sinnes which they have contracted in the world, of themselves, till a new flood, waters of repentance, drawne up, and sanctified by the Holy Ghost, worke that blessed effect in them.

JOHN DONNE: *Sermons*

We ought not to be disturbed by these truths [disturbing aspects of man's behavior], I can never understand why Christians are sometimes horrified by revelations of this kind. For example, when I meet with Christians who are scandalized by the Freudian uncovering of the seamy side of the unconscious, or perhaps by the rather dubious calculations of Mr. Kinsey, I am inclined to say at once, "But, my dear fellow, why are you surprised? I thought you believed in the Fall. The man who believes in the Fall should at least be unshockable!" It is indeed an odd paradox if a man says he believes in the Fall of man yet is shocked at anything human. Let us leave it to the romantic humanists to be shocked at these revelations. Being shocked at this kind of thing is no part of our game, so to speak.

It is strange that so many people who proclaim that they accept the orthodox belief in original sin are so little aware of the meaning and implications of their own theology that they are continually surprised and scandalized by the spectacle of the visible sins of their neighbors. After all, the visible sins are no more than the outward manifestation of the underlying sinfulness, and the orthodox Christian should not be particular shocked or surprised by their evidence.

Similarly, as we come to know more about the sins and sinfulness concealed in the lower depths of the human mind, the Christian should accept this new knowledge as a further confirmation of his own theological beliefs, neither surprising nor shocking, but precisely what his theology should lead him to expect. The laconic President Coolidge's Baptist preacher was described as being against sin. But more profoundly understood, however, the essentially Christian attitude is against sinfulness rather than against sin, against the underlying causal malady rather than against outward consequences and symptoms, and in no circumstances whatsoever against the sinner.

J. V. LANGMEAD CASSERLEY: *Graceful Reason*

And what does ridiculous mean? Isn't every one constantly being or seeming ridiculous? Besides, nearly all clever people are fearfully afraid of being ridiculous, and that makes them unhappy. All I am surprised at is that you should be feeling that so early, though I've observed it for some time past, and not only in you. Nowadays the very children have begun to suffer from it. It's almost a sort of insanity. The devil has taken the form of that vanity and entered into the whole generation.

FYODOR DOSTOYEVSKY: *The Brothers Karamazov*

If one thread more than any other is woven through the stuff of Western thinking it is that man has the power and the responsibility to mold society more closely to his heart's desire. The medieval aspiration to renew all things in Christ, the Puritan belief in work and thrift as the tools of the Kingdom, the Deist and rationalist confidence in social reform and even revolution as a means of remaking society—all these philosophies are derived from the fundamental Christian roots of our society with its belief in man as a free agent, morally responsible for his neighbor and set upon earth to remold human society upon a supernatural plan. Even when, in nineteenth-century liberalism, all apparent theological overtones had vanished, the belief in man—in his freedom, responsibility, and social duty—and in the coming of a better society by his efforts still betrayed the metaphysics that had given it birth.

But in the nineteenth century, a profound change began to occur at the very basis of Western thinking. In essence, it was a return to the determinism which Christian thought had banished from the world. Determinism had, it is true, begun its reinvasion with the eighteenth-century belief in a preexistent harmony and in the "hidden law" regulating economic life. If man ought, in his economic life, to act solely as his material interests guided him, then inevitably some of the most essential elements in human society were removed from rational and moral control and handed over to the goddess Chance or Necessity, and it was only a matter of guess and faith that she was a beneficent deity and not the "savage necessity" of classical thought. But early in the nineteenth century not only economic life but also man himself were withdrawn from the arena of freedom, rationality, and moral choice and plunged into a world of material conditioning. To Feuerbach, for instance, "Man is what he eats." The physical environment into which he is born and the physical heredity with which he enters life determine his thoughts, ideals, and aspirations quite as absolutely as they do his physical needs and desires. BARBARA WARD: *Faith and Freedom*

Nothing is more obvious than the split in both our unconscious life and conscious personality. Without the help of modern psychology, Paul expressed the fact in his famous words, "For I do not do the good I desire, but rather the evil that I do not desire." And then he continued in words that might well be the motto of all depth psychology: "Now if I should do what I do not wish to do, it is not I that do it, but rather sin which dwells within me." The apostle sensed a split between his conscious will and his real will, between himself and something strange within and alien to him. He was estranged from himself; and that estrangement he called "sin." He also called it a strange "law in his limbs," an irresistible compulsion. How often we commit certain acts in perfect consciousness, yet with the shocking sense that we are being controlled by an alien power! That is the experience of the separation of ourselves from ourselves, which is to say "sin," whether or not we like to use that word.

PAUL TILLICH: *The Shaking of the Foundations*

The Bible is not like a book of edification, telling us many stories of men's temptations and their overcoming. To be precise, the Bible tells only two temptation stories, the temptation of the first man and the temptation of Christ, that is the temptation which led to man's fall, and the temptation which led to Satan's fall. All other temptations in human history have to do with those two stories of temptation. Either we are tempted in Adam or we are tempted in Christ. Either the Adam in me is tempted—in which case we fall. Or the Christ in us is tempted—in which case Satan is bound to fall.

The temptation of the first man presents the enigma of the tempter in paradise. We are very prone to look behind that happening over which the mystery of the unrevealed must lie, namely the origin of the tempter. From that happening in paradise we learn three things.

First, that the tempter is to be found wherever there is innocence. Indeed the tempter is only to be found where there is innocence; for where there is guilt, he has already gained power.

Second, it is the quite unmediated appearance of the tempter in the voice of the serpent in paradise, the presence of Satan in paradise—in no way established or justified (not even by any philosophy about Lucifer)—which brings out his character as a seducer. It is the same inscrutable, contingent suddenness of which we spoke before. The voice of the tempter does not come out of an abyss only recognized as "Hell." It completely conceals its origin. It is suddenly near me and speaks to me. In paradise it is the serpent—quite plainly a creature of God—through whom the tempter speaks to Eve. Indeed there is no sign of the origin of the tempter in fire and brimstone. The denial of the origin belongs to the essence of the seducer.

Third, in order, however, to win access to innocence, it is necessary that the denial of origin should be maintained until the end. Innocence means clinging to the Word of God with pure, undivided hearts. Thus the tempter must introduce himself in the name of God. He bears with him the Word of God and expounds it: "Ought God to have said?" Have you understood God, the Lord, rightly here? Ought not another construction to be put on his Word? We cannot imagine the nameless dread which must have beset the first man in the face of such a possibility. In front of innocence yawns the abyss of yet unknown guilt; in front of faith the abyss of unknown doubts; in front of life the abyss of yet unknown death. This dread belonging to innocence, which the devil will rob of its only strength, the Word of God, is the sin of the seduction. It is not a question of engaging in a struggle, of the freedom of decision for good or for evil—it is not concerned with the ethical concept of seduction. Rather is Adam delivered up defenceless to the tempter. He lacks every insight, power, perception, which would have equipped him for the struggle with his adversary. He is left quite alone. The abyss has opened up beneath him. Only one thing remains: in the midst of this abyss he is upheld by the hand of God, by God's Word. Thus, in the hour of temptation, Adam can only shut his eyes and stand and let himself be upborne by the grace of God. But Adam falls. "Ought God to have said?" In the abyss of this question Adam sinks and with him the whole of mankind. From the time of Adam's expulsion from paradise every man is born with this question, which Satan has put in Adam's heart. That is the first question of all flesh: "Ought God to have said?" By this question all flesh comes to fall. The seduction of Adam brings all flesh to death and condemnation.

DIETRICH BONHOEFFER: *Temptation*

This person . . . is a unique being in the eyes of God, and when he forgets who he is his uniqueness becomes aloneness, and in terror of his aloneness he seeks security in the religion of collective man or in the religion of race and nation, or he shouts his defiance into the gathering dark, or he consoles himself that science, having split the atom and created life, will soon turn its attention to himself and bring him—chief joy of his desiring—quietness and peace of mind. Or, most terrible of all, he will, as in Budd Schulberg's well-known novel, *The Disenchanted,* shatter the image of God: life will mean benzedrine, and sleep will mean nembutal, and happiness will mean alcohol, and love will mean promiscuity. What other word is there than redemption? What other way, than to know who we are, persons unique in the eyes of God, with a freedom that can never be absolute, a freedom that can only be realized when we understand and obey the conditions of freedom?

ALAN PATON: "The Person in Community,"
The Christian Idea of Education

... **Your generation is suffering** from what for a lack of a better word I shall call *over-debunk*. There was a lot of debunking that had to be done, of course. Bigotry, militarism, nationalism, religious intolerance, hypocrisy, phonyness, all sorts of dangerous, ready-made, artificially preserved false values. But your generation and the generation before yours went too far with their debunking job. You went overboard. Over-debunk, that's what you did. It's moral overkill. It's like those insecticides Rachel Carson speaks of in her book, that poison everything, and kill all the nice, useful bugs as well as the bad ones, and in the end poison human beings as well. In the end, it poisons life itself, the very air we breathe. That's what you did, morally and intellectually speaking. Yours is a silent spring. You have over-protected yourselves. You are all no more than twenty, twenty-two years old, but yours is a silent spring, I'm telling you. Nothing sings for you any more. You were so angry with all the dangerous, phony piper's tunes that you ended up by breaking all the pipes and hating all the tunes. You have reduced the world to a spiritual shambles. God is ha-ha-ha. The soul is ho-ho-ho. Booze is reality. Love is sex. Family—what's that, are you kidding? So all you have left now is the H-bomb. That at least gives you a purpose in life. To be against it, I mean. You've got something to live for, or to live against ... but suppose the Russians and the Americans suddenly agree to get rid of the bomb? What then? You will be left with nothing. ... I shall say one more word. ...

—Oh, Godlessness! ...

—That's right, the Dominican said. Oh, Godlessness. But the point is: you don't seem to enjoy it. Something is still missing, eh? You got rid of God and, isn't that funny, something is still missing. Perhaps you ought to try to get rid of yourselves a little. Perhaps you will end up by getting rid of yourselves as well. I would begin by that, if I were you ... [there is] A riddle, I think you call it in English. Yes, a riddle. You probably know it, it comes from some sort of American children's game. The question is: "Who took the cookie from the cookie jar?" ... I see you know the game. Very interesting. You are all very bright and clever so maybe you'll find an answer. Who took the cookie from the cookie jar indeed. Well, maybe science did it, or maybe Freud did it, or maybe Marx did it. Or maybe prosperity, materialism. Hard-boiled realism and rationalism. I don't know and I don't care. But you certainly seem to be missing the cookie very much. You twist and turn and ache looking for it. That's one way of admitting its existence, it seems to me. . . .

ROMAIN GARY: The Ski Bum

The religious man . . . is thoroughly realist, not escapist at all. He sees life's horrors, and he confesses life's sin. He shares life's sorrows, he suffers life's pain, he moves on through life to certain death. He does not pretend that these are illusions, and he does not expect to find any way of passing them by. But he does not dwell on horror for horror's sake, nor does he journey to death in any morbidity of spirit. His attention, still and always, is on values, and his consecration is to the values in which as a religious person he believes.

Here the charge of escapism breaks down flatly and finally. Its very making, in the light of the history of religious leadership and religious loyalty, is evidence of the deepest historical ignorance. So far from escaping the unpleasant realities of life, or thinking to make light of them, the religious man by his very devotion may bring upon himself greatly increased suffering, and though not a more certain death certainly an earlier and more painful one.

GEORGE HEDLEY: *The Superstitions of the Irreligious*

One of the really surprising things about the present bewilderment of humanity is that the Christian Church now finds herself called upon to proclaim the old and hated doctrine of sin as a gospel of cheer and encouragement. The final tendency of the modern philosophies—hailed in their day as a release from the burden of sinfulness—has been to bind man hard and fast in the chains of an iron determinism. The influence of heredity and environment, of glandular make-up and the control exercised by the unconscious, of economic necessity and the mechanics of biological development, have all been invoked to assure man that he is not responsible for his misfortunes and therefore not to be held guilty. Evil has been represented as something imposed upon him from without, not made by him from within. The dreadful conclusion follows inevitably, that as he is not responsible for evil, he cannot alter it; even though evolution and progress may offer some alleviation in the future, there is no hope for you and me, here and now. I well remember how an aunt of mine, brought up in an old-fashioned liberalism, protested angrily against having continuously to call herself a "miserable sinner" when reciting the Litany. Today, if we could really be persuaded that we *are* miserable sinners—that the trouble is not outside us but inside us, and that therefore, by the grace of God we can do something to put it right, we should receive that message as the most hopeful and heartening thing that can be imagined.

DOROTHY L. SAYERS: *Creed or Chaos*

The Church, at any rate, says that man's will is free, and that evil is the price we pay for knowledge, particularly the kind of knowledge which we call self-consciousness. It follows that we can, by God's grace, do something about the pattern. Moreover, God Himself, says the Church, is doing something about it—with our cooperation, if we choose, in despite of us if we refuse to cooperate—but always, steadily, working the pattern out.

DOROTHY L. SAYERS: *Creed or Chaos*

The Self and Sin

From the evidence to be found in certain distant periods of history, it would seem that the idea of God was then so overwhelming that it left no room for pride of self or even for much consideration of it. The language about the self is undeveloped, and its rights and claims remain in the background. Gradually the status of the self was recognized, and the light which enabled its substance and function and dignity to be fully seen came from a divine source. Moved by this vision of his own powers, man proceeded to his conquest over nature and to a preoccupation with his own problems and the problems of society. The position was reversed, and instead of the idea of God filling the sky, it was now the idea of man, and the thought of God dimmed. The effect of this change has taken time to show itself, and it is unexpected. Now that the idea of God has dipped below the horizon, man has ceased to be able to see himself and what he is or should be.

MARTIN C. D'ARCY: *No Absent God*

A **person** may be thoroughly "devoted" to a cause, a community, or a creative relationship, and yet he may, within terms of that devotion, express his final concern for his own prestige or power or security. This bondage of the will to the interests of the self is what is meant by the "bondage of the will" in Christian theory.

REINHOLD NIEBUHR: *The Self and the Dramas of History*

Justice, power, and love towards oneself is rooted in the justice, power, and love which we receive from that which transcends us and affirms us. The relation to ourselves is a function of our relation to God.

PAUL TILLICH: *Love, Power, and Justice*

Sin centers life's meaning in the self and in things about which the self cares most. But do we add with full seriousness: "Who then can be saved?" What, in your life and mine, is not, in some sense, a worldly attachment?

To be sure, Christians are not forbidden to cherish authentic goods in this life—bodily health, the blessings of home, productive work, communal order, world peace. What monsters we would be if we failed to cherish these things! But the Christian is bidden to look beyond them all. Not because we know, with a fatalistic wisdom, that any one of them can be taken from us, but because to fail to look beyond them is to forget the source. Sin, at its roots, is ingratitude. It is a sort of seizure of life, as though by right, instead of the receiving of a gift.

DAVID E. ROBERTS: *The Grandeur and Misery of Man*

I will tell you instead, gentlemen, another interesting and rather characteristic anecdote of Ivan Fyodorovitch himself. Only five days ago, in a gathering here, principally of ladies, he solemnly declared in argument that there was nothing in the whole world to make men love their neighbours. That there was no law of nature that man should love mankind, and that, if there had been any love on earth hitherto, it was not owing to a natural law, but simply because men have believed in immortality. Ivan Fyodorovitch added in parenthesis that the whole natural law lies in that faith, and that if you were to destroy in mankind the belief in immortality, not only love but every living force maintaining the life of the world would at once be dried up. Moreover, nothing then would be immoral, everything would be lawful, even cannibalism. That's not all. He ended by asserting that for every individual, like ourselves, who does not believe in God or immortality, the moral law of nature must immediately be changed into the exact contrary of the former religious law, and that egoism, even to crime, must become, not only lawful, but even recognized as the inevitable, the most rational, even honorable outcome of his position.

FYODOR DOSTOYEVSKY: *The Brothers Karamazov*

It is, however, a power to endure hardship, not a way to avoid it, that authentic Christianity holds God to give. Escape from suffering is not promised to them who would follow the Christ. What is promised is victory over suffering, in the conviction that the moment's personal affliction weighs but little in the scale of everlasting values.

Christianity, therefore, along with its parent Judaism, has been realistic from the beginning; and about the darker sides of life as well as the bright ones. With characteristic inconsistency those who blame the Christian Church for offering psychic escape, damn it at the same time for producing a "guilt complex" by its emphasis upon the sinfulness of man. St. Paul and St. John never heard of complexes, but they were realistic practical psychologists, and they knew how fallible they and all men were. They knew, too, that their fallibility, and all men's, threatened the survival of any good in them or in their world. "O wretched man that I am!" cries the apostle to the Gentiles; "who shall deliver me from the body of this death?" "If we say that we have no sin," warns the Ephesian interpreter, "we deceive ourselves, and the Truth is not in us."

GEORGE HEDLEY: *The Superstitions of the Irreligious*

On all these essentials in the understanding of the self we may expect to find considerable agreement between the classical atheist and the classical Christian. The cardinal point is that the self is not known subjectively; it is known objectively. It is not found in introspection. It is found in those extroverted interests, loyalties, and loves which, in one way or another, are located in Society, Humanity, Nature, and God. Where there are no such interests and loyalties and commitments, there simply is no self.

Socrates is an epitome of all that is said here. Nothing is more scandalous than the effort to assimilate him to the existentialists. He had none of the sickly modern interest in one's private feelings and attitudes. It is true that he said, "Know thyself." True also that, when he looked for his self, he practiced what he believed to be the method of recollection. Nevertheless, what he was finally looking for were certain eternal and objective Ideas and Ideals which he believed to be constitutive not only of himself but of the whole universe. It was in devotion to such Ideals that he ordered his career, and it was in confidence that some part of him must be immortal like the Ideals with which he had lived that he died serene.

ROBERT ELLIOT FITCH:
The Odyssey of the Self-Centered Self

Greater than faith and hope, we are told, is love. Of all false loves, that which is most false is love of the self. Proper titles for this sort of love are Egotism, Selfishness, Pride. In its most dynamic expression, Pride, it has been studied by philosophers, theologians, and moralists, and presented by dramatists like Sophocles, Shakespeare, and Corneille. Yet the love of self is an enduring love, and today enters into a kind of crepuscular "scientific" phase in the teaching of Carl Rogers and of Erich Fromm. For this cult we have set before us a new commandment: "Thou shalt love thy Self with all thy heart and with all thy soul and with all thy mind. This is the first and great commandment." If by chance there should be any energy or leisure left over after we carry out this most engrossing of all occupations, then a second commandment may be in order: "Thou shalt love thy neighbor as thyself." Some persons might wish to add, as an afterthought, "Thou shalt love the Lord thy God, too." But the third commandment is tautologous, for the Lord my God is Me.

ROBERT ELLIOT FITCH:
The Odyssey of the Self-Centered Self

As the rake begins with his self, so will he end with his self. Whether he is in love with himself, or sick of himself, or just feeling sorry for himself, he is unable, as rake, ever to apprehend any reality other than that of his own ego. This is his prison. This is the hell from which there is for him, on his own terms, forever no exit.

ROBERT ELLIOT FITCH:
The Odyssey of the Self-Centered Self

If one asks what the self is, the answer is that it is its interests, its activities, its loves. Aristotle and John Dewey would prefer the first two terms—interests and activities. Saint Paul and Martin Luther would prefer the third term—love. Spinoza would approve of them all. The modern expression would be commitments. While these terms differ from each other to some degree, they do not differ in direction and intent. Maybe there is more ardor in love, more intelligence in an interest. Aristotle would remind us that there are levels of interest and of activity: the vegetable interest in food and in reproduction; the animal interest in motion and in sensation; the human interest in reason. A Christian would remind us also of the order of our loves: a supervening love of God, and, in genetic order, a love of self, of family, of community, of country, of humanity—all of which loves take quality and power from the larger love of God. In any case the interests and loves of the self are directed, not to itself, but to outer objects. The self is created and is found in these objective interests, activities, and loves.

ROBERT ELLIOT FITCH:
The Odyssey of the Self-Centered Self

The Christian cannot elude ethics on his way to the sanctuary of God. Over against the contrite acknowledgement of our own faultiness, our ingrained egotism and turbulent desires, the Church sets the Acknowledgement of our responsibility, and the bracing appeal to the moral will. Humility does not mean an easy acquiescence in our own shabbiness. The human nature which is to be offered at the altar for God's purpose, must be ordered and purified, in so far as man is able to do it. He must at least set his life in order as well as he can, submit thought, word and deed to the judgement of Love before he goes further. "Let a man examine himself," says St. Paul to those who come to the Christian mysteries. Not as to whether he is good enough, for this question is not worth asking; but as to whether he is willing to take trouble enough, whether his face is set towards Eternity, and whether the demands and interests of the Eternal are given priority over the demands and interests of self-will. Self-conquest in its most realistic and costly form is asked of the Christian communicant. A purely mystical religion, leaving the sense-world behind in its flight towards God, might elude all this; but an incarnational religion never can. It must unify and carry forward humanity in its wholeness in its approach to the altar of God.

EVELYN UNDERHILL: *An Anthology of the Love of God*

The lie is the specific evil which man has introduced into nature. All our deeds of violence and our misdeeds are only as it were a highly-bred development of what this and that creature of nature is able to achieve in its own way. But the lie is our very own invention, different in kind from every deceit that the animals can produce. A lie was possible only after a creature, man, was capable of conceiving the being of truth. It was possible only as directed against the conceived truth. In a lie the spirit practises treason against itself.

MARTIN BUBER: *Good and Evil*

Before I commit a sin it seems to me so shallow, that I may wade through it dry-shod from any guiltiness. But when I have committed it, it often seems so deep that I cannot escape without drowning. Thus I am always in the extremities; either my sins are so small that they need not my repentance, or so great that they cannot obtain thy pardon. Lend me, O Lord, a reed out of thy Sanctuary, truly to measure the dimension of my offences. But oh! as thou revealest to me more of my misery, reveal also more of thy mercy.

THOMAS FULLER: *Good Thoughts in Bad Times*

The sixth Deadly Sin is named by the Church *Acedia* or *Sloth*. In the world it calls itself Tolerance; but in hell it is called Despair. It is the accomplice of the other sins and their worst punishment. It is the sin which believes in nothing, cares for nothing, seeks to know nothing, interferes with nothing, enjoys nothing, loves nothing, hates nothing, finds purpose in nothing, lives for nothing, and only remains alive because there is nothing it would die for. We have known it far too well for many years. The only thing perhaps that we have not known about it is that it is mortal sin.

DOROTHY L. SAYERS: *Creed or Chaos*

The word "punishment" for sin has become so corrupted that it ought never to be used. But once we have established the true doctrine of man's nature, the true nature of judgment becomes startlingly clear and rational. It is the inevitable consequence of man's attempt to regulate life and society on a system that runs counter to the facts of his own nature. In the physical sphere, typhus and cholera are a judgment on dirty living; not because God shows an arbitrary favoritism to nice, clean people, but because of an essential element in the physical structure of the universe. In the state, the brutal denial of freedom to the individual will issue in a judgment of blood, because man is so made that oppression is more intolerable to him than death. The avaricious greed that prompts men to cut down forests for the speedy making of money brings down a judgment of flood and famine, because that sin of avarice in the spiritual sphere runs counter to the physical law of nature. We must not say that such behavior is wrong because it does not pay; but rather that it does not pay because it is wrong. As T. S. Eliot says: "A wrong attitude towards nature implies, somewhere, a wrong attitude towards God, and the consequence is an inevitable doom."

DOROTHY L. SAYERS: *Creed or Chaos*

The universal moral *law* (or natural law of humanity) is discoverable, like any other law of nature, by experience. It cannot be promulgated, it can only be ascertained, because it is a question not of opinion but of fact. When it has been ascertained, a moral *code* can be drawn up to direct human behavior and prevent men, as far as possible, from doing violence to their own nature. No code is necessary to control the behavior of matter, since matter is apparently not tempted to contradict its own nature, but obeys the law of its being in perfect freedom. Man, however, does continually suffer this temptation and frequently yields to it. This contradiction within his own nature is peculiar to man, and is called by the Church "sinfulness"; other psychologists have other names for it.

DOROTHY L. SAYERS: *The Mind of the Maker*

Once upon a time there was a peasant woman and a very wicked woman she was. And she died and did not leave a single good deed behind. The devils caught her and plunged her into the lake of fire. So her guardian angel stood and wondered what good deed of hers he could remember to tell God; "she once pulled up an onion in her garden," said he, "and gave it to a beggar woman." And God answered: "You take that onion then, hold it out to her in the lake, and let her take hold and be pulled out. And if you can pull her out of the lake, let her come to Paradise, but if the onion breaks, then the woman must stay where she is." The angel ran to the woman and held out the onion to her; "Come," he said, "catch hold and I'll pull you out." And he began cautiously pulling her out. He had just pulled her right out, when the other sinners in the lake, seeing how she was being drawn out, began catching hold of her so as to be pulled out with her. But she was a very wicked woman and she began kicking them. "I'm to be pulled out, not you. It's my onion, not yours." As soon as she said that, the onion broke. And the woman fell into the lake and she is burning there to this day.

FYODOR DOSTOYEVSKY: *The Brothers Karamazov*

Man and Man

Remember particularly that you cannot be a judge of any one. For no one can judge a criminal, until he recognizes that he is just such a criminal as the man standing before him, and that he perhaps is more than all men to blame for that crime. When he understands that, he will be able to be a judge.

FYODOR DOSTOYEVSKY: *The Brothers Karamazov*

Lovers or friends desire two things. The one is to love each other so much that they enter into each other and only make one being. The other is to love each other so much that, with half the globe between them, their union will not be diminished in the slightest degree. All that man vainly desires here below is perfectly realized in God. We have all those impossible desires within us as a mark of our destination and they are good for us when we no longer hope to accomplish them.

SIMONE WEIL: *Waiting for God*

In much of Eastern philosophy, the greater stress seems to be on ridding the soul of all desire so that no obstacle may hold it back from absorption into infinite nothingness: the world is a snare from which the spirit must be loosed. In Christ's teaching, the emphasis is not on the absence of desire but on the direction of desire into the right channels—away from self-love and toward God, who alone is the Good, and toward our neighbor whom we love for God's sake. The world is not evil: we are bidden to consider the lilies of the field and to take delight and instruction from homely things—from the shepherd who discovers his lost sheep or the housewife who sweeps up her lost penny. But the natural order is darkened by sin and can be redeemed and used rightly only by those who seek first the kingdom of heaven. St. Augustine's phrase, "Love God and do what you like," expresses the safety of the world for those whose desires are rightly ordered.

BARBARA WARD: *Faith and Freedom*

In general the devil operates on the assumption that the more beautiful and God-blessed anything is, the more useful it can prove to him. Reasoning thus, he works to persuade the husband and wife that marriage is so complete a fulfillment as to obviate the need for any other temple than their home. He teaches each to regard the other as good enough. If he succeeds, they begin—quite literally—to "idolize" each other.

This form of religion—like many other forms—delights the devil more than any amount of atheism. He agrees with the Bible, which solemnly warns time and again against idolatry, but is almost silent in regard to atheism. And the devil prefers that idolatry be on a high level. He knows that a confirmed alcoholic may some day wake up in revulsion and join Alcoholics Anonymous. But if a man's wife truly reflects the radiance and glory of her Creator, if she deserves a love separated only by a hair's-breadth from idolatry, can her husband be expected to arise some morning with disgust in his heart and organize Idolaters Anonymous?

"God, Thou art here—and this is Thine—but this is not Thou." These three cries need to be uttered often and with equal emphasis; they are passwords to spiritual health—and not alone in marriage. The nature lover needs to say them to nature, the social reformer to his work of reform.

CHAD WALSH: *Behold the Glory*

The friendship between the I and the Thou achieves its consummation only when God is the invisible Third in whose presence we both stand, the invisible point of intersection through which all the lines must pass which run, this way and that, between us. Marriage is happy only if both husband and wife are sustained by God, so that each is able to support and uphold the other. One human being can receive the confidence of another, and be a person to whom he can speak his mind unreservedly and in all situations, only if he accepts a priestly responsibility for him before God. If that is not the case, then he lacks all pastoral authority and the whole relation of trust rests only on a human power of suggestion which he exerts upon the other. This power of suggestion may at any moment fail if the veil is torn and the other sees that it was all a mere deception. Thus all the relations in which human beings afford one another mutual support always rest solely on the fact that God sustains them all, because He is the ultimate Thou of them all. All true relations of confidence between human beings are governed by the principle *teneo quia teneor:* I hold because I am held.

KARL HEIM: *Christian Faith and Natural Science*

Hierarchism is a vital need of the human soul. It is composed of a certain veneration, a certain devotion toward superiors, considered not as individuals, nor in relation to the powers they exercise, but as symbols. What they symbolize is that realm situated high above all men and whose expression in this world is made up of the obligations owed by each man to his fellow men. A veritable hierarchy presupposes a consciousness on the part of the superiors of this symbolic function and a realization that it forms the only legitimate object of devotion among their subordinates. The effect of true hierarchism is to bring each one to fit himself morally into the place he occupies.

SIMONE WEIL: *The Need for Roots*

Forgive us our virtues
As we forgive those who are virtuous against us.

CHAD WALSH: *The Psalm of Christ*

In the eyes of him who takes his stand in love, and gazes out of it, men are cut free from their entanglement in bustling activity. Good people and evil, wise and foolish, beautiful and ugly, become successively real to him; that is, set free they step forth in their singleness, and confront him as *Thou*. In a wonderful way, from time to time, exclusiveness arises—and so he can be effective, helping, healing, educating, raising up, saving. Love is responsibility of an *I* for a *Thou*. In this lies the likeness—impossible in any feeling whatsoever—of all who love, from the smallest to the greatest and from the blessedly protected man, whose life is rounded in that of a loved being, to him who is all his life nailed to the cross of the world, and who ventures to bring himself to the dreadful point—to love *all men*.

MARTIN BUBER: *I and Thou*

«3» The Secular Challenge

The heart of the appeal of Marxism lies in its mystique of history. Before everything else it is a substitute for Christianity—a dogmatic scheme in terms of which those who are prevented by the presuppositions of the secular outlook from believing in Christianity can nevertheless accept and express something like the Biblical philosophy of life and history, giving them a sense of purpose and direction and self-transcending worth, an experience of generous emotions and moral ideas akin to those which Christianity inspires. Against a fundamentally religious propaganda of this kind, a merely secular liberalism must inevitably prove powerless in the last resort. The wave of secular and skeptical liberalism that has swept across the Western world since the eighteenth century has created a tragic void in the Western soul. For great multitudes it has emptied the religious dimension of life of all content. The merely secular liberals in effect desire that this spiritual vacuum should continue as such indefinitely, but that is impossible. If Christianity is gone something must take its place and that something is more likely to be communism than anything else. On the intellectual and spiritual plane, therefore, the most important way of opposing communism is to level an unceasing attack against the secular outlook on life, an attack that aims at exposing the hollowness and unreality of its presuppositions and characteristic modes of existence. There would be very little temptation to believe in Marxism if modern men and women could only be delivered from the misleading—and, logically speaking, quite unnecessary—prejudices and attitudes that make it impossible for them to believe in Christianity. Who would relish the insipid substitute if he was capable of digesting the natural food? Thus Christian preachers, poets, novelists, journalists, and philosophers are in the very front line of the anti-communist struggle, whether they care for the situation or not, because their existence and witness is a living demonstration that the secular point of view is not, as has been widely supposed, the only outlook possible for modern men.

But the Christianity we have now in mind is the downright dogmatic and institutional Christianity, a Christianity equipped, so to speak, to survive the rough and tumble of human history, a revealed and proclaimed gospel, not an idealistic aspiration. A merely moralistic, liberal Christianity of noble purposes and high ideals of personal integrity cannot help or sustain us at such a time as this. We have to recover the power to believe in the genuine Biblical and creedal Christianity, a Christianity that is as much a dogma about history as Marxism itself, a revelation of the power and purpose of the forces that preside over human destiny. To me, quite frankly, this seems the only kind of Christianity worth having, the only kind worth the infinite mental and moral strain and effort exacted by the process of living it, and the endless expenditure of time and breath and words and paper and ink consumed in the process of propagating it. Some such dogma about life and history men must have, and also some institutional channels through which it can find expression. These the communists provide. The West will strive against them in vain unless it knows and resorts to better ones.

J. V. LANGMEAD CASSERLEY: *The Bent World*

The struggle between the prophetic religion of the living God and the doctrine of loyalty to the state as the highest of all loyalties, before which every other loyalty must give way, is clearly and unforgettably set out in the great myths that constitute the narrative portions of the Book of Daniel. The principle laid down in that book is clear: those who know that the supreme loyalty and moral obligation of man is to be found in the sphere of his relationship to the living God, and that to this loyalty every secular loyalty whatsoever must defer, cannot conceivably worship any emperor or state or temporal political reality. Loyalty to God in and through the life of the Church takes precedence of any possible loyalty to state and nation.

J. V. LANGMEAD CASSERLEY: *The Bent World*

The human heart has both appetites and despairs which rational codes alone are unable to control. Man is lonely. He is not self-sufficient. He rebels against meaninglessness in life. He is haunted by death. He is afraid. He needs to feel himself part of a wider whole and he has unassuageable powers of dedication and devotion which must find expression in worship and service. If therefore, there is no other outlet for these powers, then the community in which he lives, the tribe, the state, Caesar, the dictator, become the natural and inevitable objects of his religious zeal. Religion is not abolished by the "abolition" of God; the religion of Caesar takes its place. And since, for a few men, the need to worship is satisfied in *hubris,* in the worship of the self, the multitudes who look for a god can nearly always be certain of finding a willing candidate. In times of crisis, when insecurity, anxiety, loneliness, and the meaninglessness of life become well nigh insupportable— how can a man tolerate years without work in modern industrial society?—the hunger for god-like leadership, for religious reassurance, for a merging of the self in the security of the whole becomes irresistible. Even when faith in God survives, the desire wells up for strong government. Where religious faith has vanished, all the energies of the soul are poured into the one channel of political faith. In our own day, Communism and National Socialism have proved to be powerful religions and have brought back into the world the identification of state and church, city and temple, king and god which made up the monolithic unity of archaic society and the universal servitude of archaic man.

Few deny the historical role of Christianity in creating a double order of reality and a division of power out of which the possibility of freedom has grown. Even the most doubtful must confront the fact that totalitarian government in its extremest form has returned when the waning of religion left the altars of the soul empty and turned men back to the oldest gods of all—the idols of the tribe. Nor is it easy to conceive of any means other than religious faith for preserving a genuine division of power in society; for if man is no more than the creature of his environment, and a product of his social order, on what foundations can he base claims and loyalties which go beyond the social order? From what source can he draw the strength to resist the claims of society? To what justice can he appeal beyond the dictates of the state?

The state is by nature so powerful and compelling and voracious an institution that the citizen, standing alone against it, is all but powerless. He needs counter-institutions, above all the counter-institution of the Church, which of all organized bodies alone can look Caesar in the face and claim a higher loyalty.

It is, however, one thing to argue that a recovery of faith in God is necessary as a safeguard of Western freedom. It is quite another to put forward sociological and political and historical facts as the basis for a revival of faith. Such a procedure runs the risk of resembling the hypocrisy of eighteenth-century cynics who argued that religion was good for the poor because it kept them contented. Faith is not a matter of convenience nor even—save indirectly—a matter of sociology. It is a question of conviction and dedication and both spring from one source only —from the belief in God as a fact, as the supreme fact of existence. Faith will not be restored in the West because people believe it to be useful. It will return only when they find that it is true.

BARBARA WARD: *Faith and Freedom*

But however obscure the coming of the Kingdom may seem in Jewish apocalyptic writing, there can be no doubt of the tremendous fascination it has exercised since on the imagination of mankind. The vision of injustice made good, of the poor raised to power and the proud brought low, which appears fully for the first time in Jewish thought, has made the Old Testament a revolutionary instrument in Christian and post-Christian society. The Anabaptists of Munster and Cromwell's Diggers were Old Testament men. For all his secularization, Marx himself is a great Jewish apocalyptic prophet. Certainly Communism owes its immense vitality more to its biblical vision of the mighty put down and the poor raised up than to its theories of value or its interpretation of history.

BARBARA WARD: *Faith and Freedom*

As soon as he reflected seriously he was convinced of the existence of God and immortality, and at once he instinctively said to himself: "I want to live for immortality, and I will accept no compromise." In the same way, if he had decided that God and immortality did not exist, he would at once have become an atheist and a socialist. For socialism is not merely the labor question, it is before all things the atheistic question, the question of the form taken by atheism today, the question of the tower of Babel built without God, not to mount to Heaven from earth but to set up Heaven on earth.

FYODOR DOSTOYEVSKY: *The Brothers Karamazov*

"Remember, young man, unceasingly," Father Paissy began, without preface, "that the science of this world, which has become a great power, has especially in the last century, analyzed everything divine handed down to us in the holy books. After this cruel analysis the learned of this world have nothing left of all that was sacred of old. But they have only analyzed the parts and overlooked the whole, and indeed their blindness is marvellous. Yet the whole still stands steadfast before their eyes, and the gates of hell shall not prevail against it. Has it not lasted nineteen centuries, is it not still a living, a moving power in the individual soul and in the masses of people? It is still as strong and living even in the souls of atheists, who have destroyed everything! For even those who have renounced Christianity and attack it, in their inmost being still follow the Christian idea, for hitherto neither their subtlety nor the ardor of their hearts has been able to create a higher ideal of man and of virtue than the ideal given by Christ of old. When it has been attempted, the result has been only grotesque. Remember this especially, young man, since you are being sent into the world by your departing elder. Maybe, remembering this great day, you will not forget my words, uttered from the heart for your guidance, seeing you are young, and the temptations of the world are great and beyond your strength to endure."

FYODOR DOSTOYEVSKY: *The Brothers Karamazov*

"Tell me yourself, I challenge you—answer. Imagine that you are creating a fabric of human destiny with the object of making men happy in the end, giving them peace and rest at last, but that it was essential and inevitable to torture to death only one tiny creature—that baby beating its breast with its fist, for instance—and to found that edifice on its unavenged tears, would you consent to be the architect on those conditions? Tell me, and tell the truth."

"No, I wouldn't consent," said Alyosha softly.

"And can you admit the idea that men for whom you are building it would agree to accept their happiness on the foundation of the un-expiated blood of a little victim? And accepting it would remain happy for ever?"

"No, I can't admit it, Brother," said Alyosha suddenly, with flashing eyes, "you said just now, is there a being in the whole world who would have the right to forgive and could forgive? But there is a Being and He can forgive everything, all and for all, because He gave His innocent blood for all and everything. You have forgotten Him, and on Him is built the edifice, and it is to Him they cry aloud, 'Thou art just, O Lord, for Thy ways are revealed!' "

FYODOR DOSTOYEVSKY: *The Brothers Karamazov*

The idea of progress has been refuted by the tragic events of current history. We have global wars instead of the parliament of mankind and the federation of the world. Cruel tyrannies have emerged in an era in which democracy and liberty were expected to be triumphant. And the world's enmities became the more tragic since science had given the weapons of warfare a new destructiveness through the discoveries of nuclear physics. History refuted the hopes of the past centuries because they were founded upon two erroneous beliefs. The one was that reason could be the master of interest and passion and therefore the instrument of increasingly universal interests. This was an error since reason is always intimately related to the self and is more easily the servant than the master of the self.

The other error was derived from the first. It was the mistaken belief that every triumph over nature and every consequent enhancement of human freedom would redound to the benefit of man. The error lay in regarding man's freedom over nature as unambiguously good. Yet all human freedom contains the possibilities of both creativity and destructiveness. Human history is therefore bound to develop in both dimensions to its end. Our generation has had tragic and vivid displays of this truth in the good and evil, in the increasing community, and in the increasingly lethal warfare in our experience. Thus contemporary history has refuted the too simple interpretations which have been given to both life and history by modern secularized religions. It is rather ironic that the Marxist alternative to the liberal idea of progress was closer to the Biblical apocalyptic views than were the progressive notions. It had a conception of judgment and redemption which embodied some of the paradoxes of Biblical faith. But it was even more grievously mistaken in its utopian visions than the liberal alternative, for it generated hell on earth through its dreams of heaven on earth.

REINHOLD NIEBUHR:
"The Two Sources of Western Culture,"
The Christian Idea of Education

Only human beings have an eternal destiny. Human collectives have not got one.

SIMONE WEIL: *The Need for Roots*

There are any number of signs showing that the men of our age have now for a long time been starved of obedience. But advantage has been taken of the fact to give them slavery.

SIMONE WEIL: *The Need for Roots*

Meaning or Meaninglessness

Meeting with God does not come to man in order that he may concern himself with God, but in order that he may confirm that there is meaning in the world.

MARTIN BUBER: *I and Thou*

Faith in divine Providence is the faith that nothing can prevent us from fulfilling the ultimate meaning of our existence. Providence does not mean a divine planning by which everything is predetermined, as in an efficient machine. Rather, Providence means that there is a creative and saving possibility implied in every situation, which cannot be destroyed by any event. Providence means that the daemonic and destructive forces within ourselves and our world can never have an unbreakable grasp upon us, and that the bond which connects us with the fulfilling love can never be disrupted.

PAUL TILLICH: *The Shaking of the Foundations*

The existentialists of the anti-religious type think so poorly of man, comprehend him so exclusively from below, that it is incomprehensible how the problem of knowledge, the glow of the light of Truth could ever arise. No matter how we may think of man, we are faced with the fact that he both knows the light of truth, and is plunged into the darkness of mistakes and error. . . . Deeper truth lies in the fact that the world is not meaningless and absurd, but is in a meaningless state. This world, the world as it appears to us, is a fallen world: in it death, absurd and meaningless, triumphs. Another world, that of reason and freedom, is revealed only in spiritual experience, something modern existentialists deny. We must view the meaningless and absurd world in which we live, but at the same time believe in spirit, which includes freedom, and in reason, which overcomes meaninglessness and transforms the world. This will be the triumph of the realm of Spirit over that of Caesar; the triumph of Truth, not only over falsehood, but over all the partial, fractional truths which have claimed to be of cardinal importance.

There is nothing higher than the search for, and the love of Truth. Truth, the one integral truth, is God, and to perceive Truth is to enter divine life. Substitution for the one integral, liberating truth by small, partial truths which pretend to be universal, leads to idolatry and slavery. On this basis arises scientism, something which is not at all science. All partial truths involve relationship, although not always realized, with one supreme Truth.

NICOLAS BERDYAEV: *The Realm of
Spirit and the Realm of Caesar*

If we are artists about living as well as about philosophy and literature, we shall wish to make our deaths fit symbols of the meanings by which we have lived. The fulfillment of this wish is the privilege of rare spirits. When Christ dies on the cross, or when Socrates drinks the poison, the death of each one tells us more about the meaning of the love or of the wisdom for which he lived. If one of us were to die in either of these ways, it would be as a cheap criminal or as a common suicide. It was therefore an excellent thing in a world where Providence can only be another name for Caprice that Albert Camus—like James Dean—should meet his end in the violence of an automobile accident. This is the new symbol which takes the place of the cup of Gethsemane or the cup of hemlock. And so in death as in life we show that the only point of the game is its absurdity.

Of course in this game the posture of nobility is an absurdity too. Nor may it be called a magnificent absurdity. The only fit label for it is the one that Carlyle gave to the ethics of John Stuart Mill—"heroism with its eyes out." One might be noble with a faith in God, or with a belief in Nature and its laws, or with a devotion to Humanity, or with a dedication to one's own Society and native land. But to be noble with a solitary self that one no longer apprehends except as a repository for depravity and death, this is the ultimate in idiocy. Though, to be sure, in this sort of world, there is neither the sane nor the absurd, neither the rational nor the irrational, for all things are the same things, and all things are nothing.

In any case let us speak no more of a "post-Christian era." This era is no more post-Christian, than post-Buddhist, or post-Moslem, or post-Judaic. But it is the post-humanist era. Atheism is now at the end of its tether.

ROBERT ELLIOT FITCH:
The Odyssey of the Self-Centered Self

Would God have made a world like this? Well, I think we may say that if anyone thought it up, it must have been God; we could never have done it. Fred Hoyle's lectures on the Nature of the Universe, given on the B.B.C. three years ago [1950], did more than anything else in recent years to bring home to popular imagination the astonishing picture of the world as astronomy reveals it. He says, "It is my view that man's unguided imagination could never have chanced upon such a structure as I have put before you in these talks. No literary genius could have invented a story one hundredth part as fantastic as the sober facts which have been unearthed by astronomical science." And again, "Here we are in this wholly fantastic universe with scarcely a clue as to whether our existence has any real significance."

It seems to me that the main point where Hoyle is wrong is in even expecting that mathematics, physics, and astronomy should give any clue to meaning and purpose. It is rather like trying to understand the meaning of a Beethoven quartet by analysing the physical vibrations of which it is made up. You can only know what it means by hearing it. The scientist is bound to leave out of account the fact of himself as the enquiring mind, and the fact of himself as the lover of knowledge, with an artist's eye, and maybe a mystic's heart. But he too is part of the world, and in one sense more mysterious than all the rest put together.

T. R. MILFORD: Foolishness to the Greeks

In the generic sense, everyone has a religion. Whether that religion emphasizes the supernatural or is adequately expressed in naturalistic terms is a matter of variations in kind. Fundamentally a man's religion is his concern for the meaning and purpose of his universe, and for his role in relation to that purpose. A man discovers his religion by asking two questions: What is the meaning of this world? What should I do about it? And even if the answer to the first question is "None," and the answer to the second question, "Nothing," that is his religion.

For the religious disposition, the meaning, or meaninglessness, of his universe must be concentrated in some central reality. For the philosopher it may be enough to deal in abstractions. So he may explain his world in terms of Truth and Beauty, or in terms of Caprice and Cruelty. But the religious disposition, at least in the West, is always concrete. Now there are in fact just five possible realities about which we may order our religion. These are: God, Nature, Humanity, Society, the Self. Whatever may be our view of the meaning and purpose of the universe, we shall focus those meanings and purposes on one of these five objects.

The object which we prefer is for us the central reality. It is the source of all being. It is also the final authority in any dispute about truth or value. Indeed, it is absurd to speak of rebelling against authority as though we proposed to do without it altogether. Actually we appeal from one authority to another. And—this is quite inescapable—our appeal is always to some view of one of the five objects enumerated: God, Nature, Humanity, Society, the Self. It is simply an act of intellectual honesty to acknowledge which one of these is focal in our piety.

ROBERT ELLIOT FITCH:
The Odyssey of the Self-Centered Self

To love life and men as God loves them—for the sake of their infinite
    possibilities,
to wait like Him,
to judge like Him
without passing judgment,
to obey the order when it is given
and never look back—
then He can use you—then, *perhaps,* He will use you.

And if He doesn't use you—what matter. In His hand, every moment
has its meaning, its greatness, its glory, its peace, its co-inherence.

From this perspective, to "believe in God" is to believe in yourself,
as self-evident, as "illogical," and as impossible to explain: if I can be,
then God *is.*

DAG HAMMARSKJÖLD: *Markings*

Other world religions have hints and glimpses of the operation of
the divine pity. The Hindu avatar, the Buddhist bodhisattva represent
the concept of the timeless one appearing in time to release man from
the bondage of the world. In Christianity the Incarnation contains far
more than the concept of simple deliverance. Deliverance as an end in
itself implies the worthlessness and meaninglessness of created things.
Christianity rejects this contempt for the work of God's hands. God
takes on human nature not only to repair the ravages of false choice,
but to restore humanity to its true dignity as the vehicle of supernatural
life, the "temple of the Holy Spirit." Christ, the second Adam, is the
firstborn of a new race of men who, as the spiritual kingdom is spread
on earth, will achieve a unity of nature and supernature comparable
to our present union of mind and animal nature but transcending it as
rational life transcends the sentient life below it.

These "new men," these saints and mystics, may be as obscure and
apparently powerless as the first human beings must have seemed, in
the dawn of rational life, to the larger mammals among which they
lived. Indeed, each stage of evolution would have been completely
mysterious had we not been reading the story backward. There is no
reason to suppose its next phase will be more obvious or sudden than
the last. But we can at least observe some faint analogy between the
emergence among scattered human beings of rational power and the

appearance, in the saints and mystics of the world, of more than ordinary vision and capacity. Surveying the human scene, we can at least doubt whether men of any other type—the conquerors, for instance, or the despots or the economic empire builders—seem to carry in them the smallest seed of a more than rational life.

It is thus the unique character of Christianity, among all the world religions, to have grasped not only the infinitude of the Creator but also the dynamism of His creation. For all its evil and suffering and sin, the world is rescued from the last horror—the horror of meaninglessness. History may be difficult to decipher but it is not a mindless record of violence and pride, of conquest and defeat. The effort of man to remake himself in the image of his Maker and to remake the world in the pattern of a divine order gives greatness and significance even to his failures. Since he is finite and free, he must sometimes fail. Since he has God-given reason and grace, his story is nonetheless one of slow ascent. In every other tradition, the height of vision seems to have reached no further than a static perfection or else the ultimate gulf of infinity. It is only in Christianity that Creator and creation are understood together in a dynamic relationship of freedom and love.

BARBARA WARD: *Faith and Freedom*

The Dream of Freedom

... **nothing that oppresses** is Christian. Christianity is essentially liberating.

LE FRÈRE UNTEL (JEAN-PAUL DESBIENS):
Les Insolences du Frère Untel

I tell Thee that man is tormented by no greater anxiety than to find some one quickly to whom he can hand over that gift of freedom with which the ill-fated creature is born. But only one who can appease their conscience can take over their freedom. In bread there was offered Thee an invincible banner; give bread, and man will worship Thee, for nothing is more certain than bread. But if someone else gains possession of his conscience—oh! then he will cast away Thy bread and follow after him who has ensnared his conscience. In that Thou was right. For the secret of man's being is not only to live but to have something to live for. Without a stable conception of the object of life, man would not consent to go on living, and would rather destroy himself than remain on earth, though he had bread in abundance. That is true. But what happened? Instead of taking men's freedom from them, Thou didst make it greater than ever! Didst Thou forget that man prefers peace, and even death, to freedom of choice in the knowledge of good and evil? Nothing is more seductive for man than his freedom of conscience, but nothing is a greater cause of suffering.

FYODOR DOSTOYEVSKY: *The Brothers Karamazov*

A Christian man is the most free lord of all, and subject to none; a Christian man is the most dutiful servant of all, and subject to everyone.

MARTIN LUTHER: *Concerning Christian Liberty*

Finally, for the sake of those to whom nothing can be stated so well but that they misunderstand and distort it, we must add a word in case they can understand even that. There are very many persons who, when they hear of this liberty of faith, straightway turn it into an occasion of license. They think that everything is now lawful for them, and do not choose to show themselves free men and Christians in any other way than by their contempt and reprehension of ceremonies, of traditions, of human laws; as if they were Christians merely because they refuse to fast on stated days, or eat flesh when others fast, or omit the customary prayers; scoffing at the precepts of men, but utterly passing over all the rest that belongs to the Christian religion. On the other hand, they are most pertinaciously resisted by those who strive after salvation solely by their observance of and because they fast on stated days, or abstain from flesh, or make formal prayers; talking loudly of the precepts of the Church and of the Fathers, and not caring a straw about those things which belong to our genuine faith. Both these parties are plainly culpable, in that, while they neglect matters which are of weight and necessary for salvation, they contend noisily about such as are without weight and not necessary.

How much more rightly does the Apostle Paul teach us to walk in the middle path, condemning either extreme and saying, "Let not him that eateth despise him that eateth not; and let not him which eateth not judge him that eateth" (Rom. xiv. 3)! You see here how the Apostle blames those who, not from religious feeling, but in mere contempt, neglect and rail at ceremonial observances, and teaches them not to despise, since this "knowledge puffeth up." Again, he teaches the pertinacious upholders of these things not to judge their opponents. For neither party observes towards the other that charity which edifieth. In this matter we must listen to Scripture, which teaches us to turn aside neither to the right hand nor to the left, but to follow those right precepts of the Lord which rejoice the heart. For just as a man is not righteous merely because he serves and is devoted to works and ceremonial rites, so neither will he be accounted righteous merely because he neglects and despises them . . . .

MARTIN LUTHER: *Concerning Christian Liberty*

Light does not fail because men have blinded themselves; it remains, with its own properties, while the blinded are plunged in darkness through their own fault. The light does not force itself on any man against his will; nor does God constrain a man, if he refuses to accept God's working. Therefore all who revolt from the Father's light, and who transgress the law of liberty, have removed themselves through their own fault, since they were created free and self-determining.

IRENAEUS (Second Century)

One thing that Christianity is clear about, unequivocally, is that freedom is empty and is slavery unless it is grounded in God . . . and that freedom rooted in a vacuum is chaos and anarchy. But if there is freedom rooted in God, if [as parents and teachers] we give these children a stance in God against us, you see, and they develop some responsibility in that relationship, then no earthly authority can threaten them absolutely and every earthly authority can be seen with some compassion as sinful.

This is the problem of the teen-ager disillusioned with his parents. He has to learn to see them in charity, as human fallen individuals, to begin to see them as a peer of theirs and to see that they have the same problems, the same sins, the same temptations that he has.

ALBERT T. MOLLEGEN: in *Schools and Scholarship*

Certainly there is no freedom where there is self-complacency about the truth of one's own beliefs. There is no freedom where there is ignorant and fanatical rejection of foreign ideas and ways of life. There is not freedom but demonic bondage where one's own truth is called the ultimate truth. For this is an attempt to be like God, an attempt which is made in the name of God.

PAUL TILLICH: *The New Being*

. . . Like all the idealistic emancipators in the past, once they tried to stop the rampage of liberation, you'll simply be trampled down by the mob. Because freedom can't be kept stationary. Starting with slavery, it rushes toward—ultimate anarchy! . . . There are no reins left to slow the Great Revolution, which may have started as far back as the Reformation. After crashing through repressive laws, it proceeded to resent all discipline. Having swept aside unjust ordinances, it went on to question all order. From criticizing ossified conventions, it now doubts all principles, all customs, ideals. From exposing prejudices and bigotry—to ridiculing all values. From prudishness, to disdain for all morality. In short, the grandson of the lover of liberty became a libertine . . . .

Affirm . . . . Try it in any field—morals, manners, literature, art—and watch them come running with their liberating axes. Chop, chop! As if it were a personal affront to their cleverness, their urbane cynicism, their sophistication. And if the blade or dagger doesn't work, they'll make mincemeat of you with a sneer, slander, or ridicule. Chop, chop! . . . One would think that debunking has grown stale for them, now that only the hollow shells are left standing. But no—the snipers keep roaming the ruins. Shooting at anything still seen to move—long after the battles are over.

EUGENE VALE: *Chaos Below Heaven*

Religion and Science

He that knows the secrets of nature with Albertus Magnus, or the motions of the heavens with Galileo, or the cosmography of the moon with Hevelius, or the body of man with Galen, or the nature of diseases with Hippocrates, or the harmonies in melody with Orpheus, or of poetry with Homer, or of grammar with Lily, or of whatever else with the greatest artist, he is nothing if he knows them merely for talk or idle speculation, or transient and external use. But he that knows them for value, and knows them his own, shall profit infinitely.

THOMAS TRAHERNE: *Centuries of Meditations, No. 341*

However paradoxical it may seem, I am convinced that Christianity alone made possible both positive science and technics. As long as man had found himself in communion with nature and had based his life upon mythology, he could not raise himself above nature through an act of apprehension by means of the natural sciences or technics. It is impossible for man to build railways, invent the telegraph or telephone, while living in the fear of demons. Thus for man to be able to treat nature like a mechanism, it is necessary for the demonic inspiration of nature and man's communion with it to have died out in the human consciousness.

NICOLAS BERDYAEV: *The Meaning of History*

I do not think, however, that I have even yet brought out the greatest contribution of Mediaevalism to the formation of the scientific movement. I mean the inexpugnable belief that every detailed occurrence can be correlated with its antecedents in a perfectly definite manner exemplifying general principles. Without this belief the incredible labors of scientists would be without hope. It is the instinctive conviction, vividly poised before the imagination, which is the motive power of research—that there is a secret, a secret which can be revealed. How has this conviction been so vividly implanted in the European mind? When we compare this tone of thought in Europe with the attitude of other civilizations when left to themselves, there seems but one source for its origin. It must come from the medieval insistence on the rationality of God, conceived as with the personal energy of Jehovah and with the rationality of a Greek philosopher. Every detail was supervised and ordered: the search into nature could only result in the vindication of the faith in rationality.

ALFRED NORTH WHITEHEAD: *Science and the Modern World*

As people like Herbert Butterfield and A. N. Whitehead have shown convincingly, science grew up within a Christian tradition: and for many years it was in no sense distinct or separate. The founder of science at Oxford, in the early thirteenth century, was Robert Grosseteste, author of a *Compendium Scientiarum* and later Bishop of Lincoln. He had no hesitation in saying that it was "impossible to understand Nature without experiment or describe her without geometry" (or, as we might say now, theoretical physics); and by this he implied the unity of science and faith, just as much as his distinguished pupil, the Somerset Friar Roger Bacon, whose *Opus Maius,* written at the request of Pope Clement IV, was designed to show that the new knowledge, so far from being an enemy of Christian faith, was actually an aid, even in the business of evangelizing mankind. This was because it could "assist the Church . . . by leading the mind through a study of the created works to a knowledge of the Creator." Indeed, arithmetic, even in the new Arab notation just coming into vogue, was something in the nature of a necessary study for theologians, who, he says, should "abound in the power of numbering."

C. A. COULSON: *Science and Christian Belief*

. . . **I have dwelt** at some length on these presuppositions because I believe that they help us to see the close links between science and religion. If what I have said is in any real sense true, then science is only possible in a community where certain religious views are widely held. We shall be prepared to agree with the late Archbishop Temple. "It may be too much to argue, as some students of the subject have done, that science is a fruit of Christianity, but it may safely be asserted that it can never spontaneously grow up in regions where the ruling principle of the Universe is believed to be either capricious or hostile."

So also Einstein, in some words carved about the fireplace in a room at Fine Hall, Princeton: "God who creates and is nature, is very difficult to understand, but He is not arbitrary or malicious."

C. A. COULSON: Science and Christian Belief

The greater part of our schoolboy's acceptance of science and rejection of religion springs from his unexamined belief that science accepts no presuppositions, and must therefore be superior to a Christianity which is overloaded with them. Yet this view is wholly wrong. Theodor Mommsen's famous phrase "science without presuppositions" is a hopelessly superficial description of our discipline. Think for a moment of some of the attitudes of mind with which any scientist comes to his search: there is honesty, and integrity, and hope: there is enthusiasm, for no-one ever yet began an experiment without an element of passion: there is an identification of himself with the experiment, a partisan character about his secret hope for its conclusion which not even an adverse result can wholly extinguish: there is a humility before a created order of things, which are to be received and studied: there is a singleness of mind about the search which reveals what the scientist himself may often hesitate to confess, that he does what he does because it seems exciting and it somehow fulfills a deep part of his very being: there is cooperation with his fellows, both in the same laboratory, and across the seven seas; there is patience, akin to that which kept Mme. Curie at her self imposed task of purifying eight tons of pitchblende to extract the few odd milligrams of radium: above all there is judgment—judgment as to what constitutes worthwhile research: judgment as to what is fit and suitable for publication. No wonder that a modern scientist—and no Christian either—has to say that "science cannot exist without judgments of value."

C. A. COULSON: Science and Christian Belief

The mid-twentieth century is an age which axiomatically grants truth and validity to scientific knowledge, but equally axiomatically discounts religious knowledge as mere opinion. This presents no problem to one conformed to the pervading convictions of his age. But to me, for whom the new range of reality I had come to know as a Christian was just as valid and substantial as the range of reality I knew as a physicist, it was a problem which acquired a primary importance in my thinking. I found myself increasingly concerned to try to understand the underlying reasons for this dichotomy between my own convictions and those of the world about me.

WILLIAM G. POLLARD: *Physicist and Christian*

...it is generally supposed that one first learns all about physics or Christianity, their factual matter, content, methods, and ways of knowing, and then on the basis of such knowledge decides whether he wishes to become a physicist or a Christian. In my experience this widespread popular impression is completely erroneous. I am convinced that real knowledge and understanding in either case comes well after, not before, such a decision has been made. I do not really know or understand the process by which as a young man I became interested in physics and soon decided that I wanted to be a physicist. Whatever that process was, it was not based on a knowledge of physics. On the contrary, I am convinced that until I had already made the decision to become a physicist, I could not even begin to really learn physics. In the same way the process which led me into full involvement with the Church is equally mysterious to me. It certainly was not the result of an exhaustive study of Christianity. Rather it is clear to me in retrospect that only after I had made my decision and my incorporation into the Church was nearly complete, did I have a secure enough platform on which to stand in order to grapple meaningfully or fruitfully with tough theological questions. This, however, is just another way of expressing the central theological affirmation that it is by grace, not works, that one becomes a Christian. To this affirmation I would add that it was also, in a completely analogous way, by grace, not by knowledge, that I became a physicist.

WILLIAM G. POLLARD: *Physicist and Christian*

What is and always has been our mainspring is faith. . . . To have faith always means: I decide to do it, I stake my existence on it. When Columbus started on his first voyage into the West, he believed that the earth was round and small enough to be circumnavigated. He did not merely think this was right in theory—he staked his whole existence on it. In a recent discussion of this aspect of European history Freyer has rightly referred to the old saying: *Credo ut intelligam*—"I believe in order that I may understand." In applying this idea to the voyages of discovery, Freyer introduced an intermediate term: *Credo ut agam; ago ut intelligam*—"I believe in order that I may act; I act in order that I may understand." This saying is relevant not only to the first great voyages but to the whole of Western science, and to the whole mission of the West.

WERNER HEISENBERG: in *Harper's,* May, 1958

The concepts "soul" or "life" do not occur in atomic physics, and they could not, even indirectly, be derived as complicated consequences of some natural law. Their existence certainly does not indicate the presence of any fundamental substance other than energy, but it shows only the action of other kinds of forms which we cannot match with the mathematical forms of modern atomic physics. . . . If we want to describe living or mental processes, we shall have to broaden these structures. It may be that we shall have to introduce yet other concepts.

WERNER HEISENBERG: quoted in *Science and Christian Belief,* by C. A. Coulson

All these contemporary theories are highly speculative and uncertain, but they all in one way or another take the history of nature back to a time when the next earlier stage must have had its origin outside of nature. Whichever pathway of understanding one takes, one is ultimately led to such a moment. In a universe in which the second law of thermodynamics holds there is no other way out. Along any historic path backwards in time one chooses to follow, one comes upon a sequence of irreversible transformations which ultimately leads to a beginning; to a moment, that is, at which something which had not existed in space-time takes up an existence within space-time. The history of the universe is not a tale told by an idiot which simply runs on and on. One cannot push it backwards along any route without finally coming to some event which transcends nature and thus leads out of nature toward the supernatural ground upon which the existence of all finite created things must rest. The origin and source of all that exists within space and time must ultimately be sought for outside space and time. This should have been obvious all along, but at the stage which science has now reached, it is a conclusion which can no longer be avoided even by those who would still prefer not to acknowledge it.

WILLIAM G. POLLARD: *Physicist and Christian*

It is all-important to recognize that spirit is not a reality comparable with other realities, like material, for example: spirit is reality in quite another sense. It is freedom and not being: it is a qualitative changing of the data of the world, it is creative energy which transfigures the world. Further, there is no spirit without God, as its original source. Man's spiritual experience, on which alone metaphysics can be based, is the only proof of the existence of God. The world of necessity, estrangement and hostility, of the absurd and final, is a world of limited, surface consciousness, to which infinity is inaccessible. There are other planes of the life of the world which may be revealed only to an altered consciousness. . . . But how can we reconcile with this the possibility of scientific perception? This does not in the least cause difficulty for science in the exact meaning of the word, and it calls forth no conflict. Science knows the real world in its present state, and science is not responsible for the fact that ours is a fallen world. Science seeks truth: in it the Logos is reflected. But it has definite limits, and there are questions which it not only cannot solve, but may not even put.

NICOLAS BERDYAEV: *The Realm of Spirit*
and the Realm of Caesar

If Jesus wished to put the point of God's complete sovereignty, we might have expected that He would use entirely different illustrations. We might well have supposed that Jesus would refer to the great events in world history where world empires, arising from the ocean of history, collapse back in impotence to make room for other world powers; or that He would refer to world catastrophes, where, perhaps through a single discovery or invention, the face of the earth has suddenly been transformed; and that He would point out how the Almighty stands behind these far-reaching revolutionary episodes, and guides them with His mighty hand. Such instances of God's omnipotence would seem to us to be the most impressive. Instead of this, Jesus points to the smallest and most trivial things that happen on earth as illustrations of the Father's power, as when a bird from one casual flock falls dead to the ground without anyone noticing it, or when a man loses a hair. Today, in the era of atomic research, we might say: No quantum-jump happens without your Father in heaven. The saying shines in its true light in the context of current atomic physics. Here we are facing a fundamental law which runs through the whole of creation. All events, however great, we now know to be the cumulation of decisions which occur in the infinitesimal realm.

KARL HEIM: *The Transformation of the Scientific World View*

We are now ready to see the answers to the profounder question, what is man? The physicist will describe him as a machine for doing work, the chemist as a means of converting chemical energy into other forms of energy, the biologist will speak of him as the latest—and perhaps the last—product of the evolutionary process. All three pictures—and of course there are more than three—arise from one or other of the grand conceptual schemes of science, and they reflect the religious character of all true study as we have described it before. But the Christian, making his act of reflection and his total response to his almost bewilderingly rich variety of pattern, will want to say: he is a child of God.

But we must be careful. The physicist, as such, gives only one of these answers, the chemist and biologist only one. The Christian gives them all. He can agree unreservedly with these others, and rejoice that their accounts are so splendid. He will say that he needs all these partial descriptions, these "two-dimensional" abstractions from the "three-dimensional" character of man's full stature, before he can claim to understand him properly. And as for those more puzzling questions about the control, and the use or the misuse, of man, these cannot be answered and a true response made, unless the partial descriptions are available. The religious view of man is not separate from, or contrary to, the scientific. It is the act of reflection and total response, not only to the scientific view, but to all other forms of revelation accessible to the "I" as well as to the "Me." In the development of this response and the knowledge on which it is partly based, the scientist has his own particular role—and it is an important one.

C. A. COULSON: *Science and Christian Belief*

Not every scientist is supported like Kepler by the feeling that in discovering the ways of nature he is "thinking God's thoughts after "Him," but at least the line which his curiosity pursues is always suggested to him by some perception of the significance and value of what he hopes to discover. Actually I believe it true that when science turns positivist it becomes at the same time pragmatic and utilitarian. When nature is believed to have no preordained meaning or purpose in itself, the speculative interest in it fails, and the remaining concern is only to subdue its inherent purposelessness to our own chosen ends. Yet if, in their turn, these ends of ours are not themselves informed by faith, if they are merely chosen and not prescribed, if they represent only human preferences dictated by interest instead of solemn obligations emanating from a source beyond ourselves, then science becomes a desperately dangerous tool to put in men's hands. Our religion has indeed taught us that man has dominion over nature, but it has also taught us that this dominion is to be exercised for the glory of God and the salvation of the soul, and that its use is therefore to be controlled by obedience to divinely ordained laws without consideration of convenience or comfort or material gain or even survival. Today we all live in fear and trembling lest the power which science confers should pass into the hands of men who regard no duty as unconditional and every moral standard as relative to just such parochial considerations as I have mentioned.

JOHN BAILLIE: *Natural Science and the Spiritual Life*

What Socrates was really protesting against was the attempt to assign causes for human behavior instead of giving reasons for it. I am myself wholly in sympathy with this protest. I believe that the illicit extension of the categories of natural science to the inner life of the spirit presages the final betrayal of our human birthright. I believe the Devil rejoices greatly as often as he finds me assigning natural causes for my frequent lapses from duty, as well as for my occasional conformity to it, instead of acknowledging my own freely chosen purposes. I can imagine nothing more convenient to my sloth, my selfishness, and my concupiscence than a philosophy which persuaded me, in the name of scientific outlook, to regard myself only as part of nature and as subject to none but nature's laws; nor can I imagine anything that would be more destructive of the very foundations of my humanity—and therefore, in the end, of my very science itself. After all, we are men before we are scientists, and except in the context of a full humanity our science will be little worth.

JOHN BAILLIE: *Natural Science and the Spiritual Life*

I have already said that, in turning aside from the search for final causes, the founders of modern science were far from denying all purpose to nature, their protest being only that this purpose was not open to empirical observation and accordingly had no place in strictly scientific procedure. Moreover, they were almost all of one mind as to what this purpose is. Bacon and Descartes, Copernicus, Gassendi, Galileo, Kepler, and virtually all the great seventeenth-century figures believed that the world was under the guiding hand of God, who had ordered all things for the best. They were all men of faith as well as men of science, and it was their faith that provided the comprehensive outlook on life in which their scientific researches were given so honorable a place. "I had rather," declared Bacon in a famous essay [Essay XVI], "believe all the fables of the Legend, and the Talmud, and the Alcoran, than that this universal frame is without a mind. . . . For while the mind of man looketh upon secondary causes, it may sometimes rest in them, and go no further; but when it beholdeth the chain of them, confederate and linked together, it must needs fly to Providence and Deity." This means that Socrates was after all justified in the main concern which animated him. He was wrong in his impatience with the search for secondary and mechanical causes, wrong in his desire to interpolate final causes into the chain of scientific explanation, and wrong in his belief that the details of nature could be deduced from the ideal ends which it was ordained to serve.

But he was right in his conviction that it is far more vitally important for us to know whither nature tends than to know how it works, and that our interest in its working must ultimately evaporate, if we are unable to believe that it tends toward some good. Sometimes nowadays we hear the phrase "the scientific outlook on life." But science itself produces no outlook on life. The outlook which it is made to serve is always determined for it by some judgment of value such as cannot by any magic be spirited out of its own observation of facts, some apprehension of quality which cannot be recorded on its pointer readings because it has nothing to do with quantity or measure.

JOHN BAILLIE: *Natural Science and the Spiritual Life*

The problem of miracles only causes difficulty between religion and science because it is badly presented. To present it properly it is necessary to give a definition of a miracle. To say that it is a fact contrary to the laws of nature is to say something completely devoid of significance. We do not know what the laws of nature are. We can only make suppositions in regard to them. If the laws we suppose are contradicted by facts, it shows that our supposition was at any rate in part erroneous. To say that a miracle is the effect of a particular act of volition on the part of God is no less absurd. Amidst all the events that take place, we have no right to maintain that certain of them rather than others are the result of God's will. All we know, in a general way, is that everything which happens, without any exception, is in accordance with the will of God considered as Creator; and that everything which contains at any rate a particle of pure good proceeds from the supernatural inspiration of God considered as Absolute Good. But when a saint performs a miracle, what is good is the saintliness, not the miracle. A miracle is a physical phenomenon necessitating as one of its prerequisites a total abandonment of the soul either to good or to evil.

One has to say either to good or to evil, for there are diabolical miracles. "For false Christs and false prophets shall arise, and shall show signs and wonders, to seduce, if it were possible, even the elect" (Mark 13:22); "Many will say to me in that day: Lord, Lord, have we not prophesied in thy name, and in thy name have cast out devils, and in thy name done wonderful works? And then I will profess unto

them: I never knew you; depart from me, ye that work iniquity"
(Matthew 7:22–23).

It is in no way contrary to the laws of nature that a total abandonment of the soul to either good or evil should be accompanied by
physical phenomena, which are only produced in such a case. It
would be contrary to the laws of nature if it were otherwise. For every
attitude of the human soul is accompanied by a certain particular
physical state. Sorrow is accompanied by salt water in the eyes, then
why not in certain states of mystical ecstasy, as is averred, a certain
lifting up of the body above the ground? The fact may be true or not;
it doesn't much matter. What is certain is that if the mystical ecstasy
corresponds to something real in the soul, it must be accompanied in
the body by phenomena which are not observable when the soul is in
a different state. The connection between mystical ecstasy and these
phenomena is formed by a mechanism similar to that which connects
sorrow with tears. We know nothing about the first mechanism. But
we don't know any more about the second one.

SIMONE WEIL: *The Need for Roots*

When we think of the flowering of the human intellect in the humility, patience, imagination, one-ness and splendor of modern science;
then we should agree not only that "science is a moral enterprise,"
but that it holds within itself the very stuff of religious experience.
And so, since the Order of Physical Nature is one aspect of God
showing Himself to His children, what they see and do when they
study it is most intimately bound up both with what He is, and what
they are. The schoolboy who tried to separate science and religion
was completely and utterly wrong: what he should have said was that
science was one part of religion and the splendor, the power, the
dynamic and progressive character of science are nothing but the
splendor and the power and the dynamic character of God, progres-
sively revealed to us We do them justice as we honor Him. With such
common features as these, it is entirely right that Max Planck should
end his *Scientific Autobiography* with these words: "Religion and natural science are fighting a joint battle in an incessant, never relaxing
crusade against scepticism and against dogmatism, against disbelief

and against superstition, and the rallying cry in this crusade has always been, and always will be: 'On to God.' "

C. A. COULSON: Science and Christian Belief

One final word of caution must be stated, however, before we leave this topic. Whenever science leads us outside of nature into supernature, what it gives us is at best an abstract mathematical entity incapable of being visualized or represented by any conceptual model. It does not, nor in the nature of things can it, lead us to a knowledge of God, or even to a recognition of his existence. Dimensions perpendicular to space-time, such as may represent heaven, hell, and eternity, are in themselves merely formal mathematical constructions. The transcendental reality whose several manifestations are the spectrum of elementary particles (whatever that may turn out to be) will certainly be impersonal and abstrusely mathematical. Whatever preceded the entry into history of the neutrons and protons which now inhabit space and time is likely to continue to be enigmatic or, at least, abstract and purely formal, in any science of the future. None of this is even particularly religious in character, to say nothing of leading to any kind of knowledge of God . . . we are absolutely dependent for our knowledge of God on his initiative in revealing himself to us through Israel and Christ. It is a forlorn and impossible hope which so many have today that man, working on his own initiative by means of science alone, may somehow eventually find God. All he can possibly discover in this way is something inscrutable which can only be expressed in abstract mathematics. No one can ever be led to Christ by such a route. God cannot be known by his creature man except insofar as he has chosen to reveal himself to man. But such revelation is an entirely different thing from science.

WILLIAM G. POLLARD: Physicist and Christian

Be not thou far from me, O Lord.
Psalm 22:19

I cannot gain again their innocence
And ignorance. I cannot see a cloud
Less than an airplane's height above the earth
And say, "We saw him disappear behind it;
Soon he'll return and bring a shining crowd

Of angels." No, the rocket and the sputnik,
Mount Palomar, inquire and do not find it,
That face, one face. If it is hid in space,
It is so many galaxies away
No instrument has seen and countersigned it.

If he is farther, he's no good to me.
Then I must find him anywhere I pray
And closer than the lashes of my eyes
And surer than my red heart at its beating
And wilder than a tiger on its prey

And he must have me for his Eucharist,
Digest my solitude by simple eating;
I am not whole until you take me whole,
Nor free until I scatter in your cells,
Nor saved, save lost past cheating and entreating.

CHAD WALSH: from *The Psalm of Christ*

«5» Creation and Existence

There is no soul of man in this world which cleaveth not either to the Creator or the creature. If he love the creature he loseth God, and goeth to death with that which he loveth. Such love is the beginning of travail and folly, in the middle it is languor and wretchedness, and in the end it is hate and pain.

JOHN WYCLIFFE: *The Poor Caitiff*

It would seem that the older and more conventional way of stating the cosmological proof [of the existence of God] does leave a sense of dissatisfaction among modern listeners, and some complain, perhaps irrelevantly, that the argument does not show up the force of their own convictions. This is somewhat surprising because the argument is a formulation of a spontaneous and evergreen belief that the world did not make itself, that there must be a creator. That this is so is borne out by a story told me by a person who visited Russia some years ago. He was given as a guide a Russian university student, a girl who spoke English. In the car which had been put at his disposal he asked the girl whether she believed in God. At first she gave him the usual Marxist answer. He noticed, however, that while speaking she had her eyes on the Russian chauffeur; so he made a remark in English to the chauffeur, which the latter clearly did not understand. Then he said to the girl: "You see that the chauffeur cannot understand what you are saying; so please tell me what you really think." Her answer was immediate and to this effect: "Of course there is a

God; do you think the world made itself?" This is the foundation of the cosmological argument.

MARTIN C. D'ARCY: *No Absent God*

And here we come up against the ultimate question which no theology, no philosophy, no theory of the universe has ever so much as attempted to answer completely. Why should God, if there is a God, create anything, at any time, of any kind at all? That is a real mystery, and probably the only completely insoluble mystery there is. The one person who might be able to give some sort of guess at the answer is the creative artist, and he, of all people in the world, is the least inclined even to ask the question, being accustomed to take all creative activity as its own sufficient justification.

But we may all, perhaps, allow that it is easier to believe the universe to have come into existence for some reason than for no reason at all. The Church asserts that there is a Mind which made the universe, that He made it because He is the sort of Mind that takes pleasure in creation, and that if we want to know what the Mind of the Creator is, we must look at Christ. In Him, we shall discover a Mind that loved His own creation so completely that He became part of it, suffered with and for it, and made it a sharer in His own glory and a fellow-worker with Himself in the working out of His own design for it.

That is the bold postulate that the Church asks us to accept, adding that, if we do accept it (and every theoretical scheme demands the acceptance of some postulate or other) the answers to all our other problems will be found to make sense.

DOROTHY L. SAYERS: *Creed or Chaos*

. . . the Judeo-Christian view [of the cosmic drama] looks beyond man and his self-asserted ends and aspirations and centers its attention on God, the author and creator of the drama. It takes the fact of the occurrence of this drama, the wonder that this particular universe should have been created at all, the marvel of its majestic splendor and dramatic development, as the central fact of all existence. It sees man as a creature of this creation especially endowed with the capacity to apprehend and appreciate the world of which he is a part. In this view art, music, poetry, and science have meaning and significance principally in that they are wonderfully effective vehicles for man's response to God and for his participation in the purpose of creation. In this view man is seen not from the inside in terms of what *he* desires and is capable of achieving apart from the rest of creation, but from the outside as a meaningful and crucial element in the whole cosmic process. It sees the primary significance of human life and human civilization to be just this: that God, who brought this mighty creation into existence, has so designed and ordered it that in the fullness of time the unfolding drama of its development has painstakingly brought forth within it a creature with the capacity to understand and enjoy His creation with Him; a creature by whom and through whom all creation can at long last offer praise to, and have communion with, its Author. As is so often proclaimed in the Bible, the chief end and purpose of man is to glorify God, his Maker, and to praise Him and enjoy Him forever. Or as it is so forcefully put by the psalmist, *I will praise thee; for I am fearfully and wonderfully made: marvelous are thy works.*

WILLIAM G. POLLARD: *The Cosmic Drama*

A matter which interests me is the emotional reaction of many scientific people to the choice between the Gamow theory of a single creation and Hoyle's theory of continuous creation. One is impressed by the real intolerability to some people of living in a created universe. It is a personal threat to them.

If the universe is created, it is contingent; there didn't even have to be any universe. They want to live in a universe where existence is necessary—not contingent on the will of something beyond—one which in the nature of things couldn't be otherwise. This was the Greco-Roman feeling: the necessity of the world.

I think if you get right down to it, their problem is the thought of our contingency, because if the universe is contingent and needn't have been at all, we are contingent and finite, and our whole existence as beings isn't self-explanatory.

We are creatures of that which is transcendent to us, of Him who is transcendent to us. This is what people don't want to confront—this basic status of existence in the biblical sense. This is where you get to real biblical categories, don't you see. They are there. You don't escape them.

WILLIAM G. POLLARD: in *Schools and Scholarship*

If I were asked to sum up the Christian message for our time in two words, I would say with Paul: It is the message of a "New Creation." . . . Christianity is the message of the New Creation, the New Being, the New Reality which has appeared with the appearance of Jesus who for this reason, and just for this reason, is called the Christ. For the Christ, the Messiah, the selected and anointed one is He who brings the new state of things.

PAUL TILLICH: *The New Being*

There is no creativity, divine or human, without the holy waste which comes out of the creative abundance of the heart and does not ask, "What use is this?" . . . By His death the reasonable morality of the disciples is turned into a paradox: the Messiah, the Anointed One, must waste Himself in order to become the Christ.

PAUL TILLICH: *The New Being*

The question of being is not the question of any special being, its existence and nature, but it is the question of what it means to *be*. It is the simplest, most profound, and absolutely inexhaustible question—the question of what it means to say that something *is*. This word "is" hides the riddle of all riddles, the mystery that there is anything at all.

PAUL TILLICH: *Biblical Religion
and the Search for Ultimate Reality*

. . . man is that being who asks the question of being. Therefore, every human being philosophizes, just as every human being moralizes and acts politically, artistically, scientifically, religiously. There are immense differences in degree, education, and creativity among different human beings in the exercise of these functions, but there is no difference in the character of the function itself. The child's restless question, "Why is this so; why is that not so?" and Kant's grandiose description, in his critique of the cosmological argument, of the God who asks himself, "Why am I?" are the same in substance although infinitely distinguished in form. Man is by nature a philosopher, because he inescapably asks the question of being. He does it in myth and epic, in drama and poetry, in the structure and the vocabulary of any language.

PAUL TILLICH: *Biblical Religion
and the Search for Ultimate Reality*

God created man in his own image and likeness, i.e. made him a creator too, calling him to free spontaneous activity and not to formal obedience to His power. Free creativeness is the creature's answer to the great call of its creator. Man's creative work is the fulfillment of the Creator's secret will.

NICOLAS BERDYAEV: *The Destiny of Man*

I feel that a man may be happy in this world and I know that this world is a world of imagination and vision. I see everything I paint in this world but everybody does not see alike. To the eye of a miser a guinea is far more beautiful than the sun and a bag worn with the use of money has more beautiful proportions than a vine filled with grapes. The tree which moves some to tears of joy is in the eyes of others only a green thing which stands in the way. As a man is so he sees.

When the sun rises, do you not see a round disk of fire something like a gold piece? O no, no, I see an innumerable company of the Heavenly host crying "Holy, Holy, Holy, is the Lord God Almighty." I do not question my bodily eye any more than I would question a window concerning sight. I look through it and not with it.

WILLIAM BLAKE (1757–1827)

The common man labors under a delusion that for the Christian, matter is evil and the body is evil. For this misapprehension, St. Paul must bear some blame, St. Augustine of Hippo a good deal more, and Calvin a very great deal. But so long as the Church continues to teach the manhood of God and to celebrate the sacraments of the Eucharist and of marriage, no living man should dare to say that matter and body are not sacred to her. She must insist strongly that the whole material universe is an expression and incarnation of the creative energy of God, as a book or a picture is the material expression of the creative soul of the artist. For that reason, all good and creative handling of the material universe is holy and beautiful, and all abuse of the material universe is a crucifixion of the body of Christ. The whole question of the right use to be made of art, of the intellect, and of the material resources of the world is bound up in this. Because of this, the exploitation of man or of matter for commercial uses stands condemned, together with all debasement of the arts and perversions of the intellect. If matter and the physical nature of man are evil, or if they are of no importance except as they serve an economic system, then there is nothing to restrain us from abusing them as we choose—nothing, except the absolute certainty that any such abuse will eventually come up against the unalterable law and issue in judgment and destruction. In these as in all other matters we cannot escape the law; we have only the choice of fulfilling it freely by the way of grace or willy-nilly by the way of judgment.

DOROTHY L. SAYERS: *Creed or Chaos*

For every work *(or act)* of creation is threefold, an earthly trinity to match the heavenly.

First, *(not in time, but merely in order of enumeration)* there is the Creative Idea, passionless, timeless, beholding the whole work complete at once, the end in the beginning: and this is the image of the Father.

Second, there is the Creative Energy *(or Activity)* begotten of that idea, working in time from the beginning to the end, with sweat and passion, being incarnate in the bonds of matter: and this is the image of the Word.

Third, there is the Creative Power, the meaning of the work and its response in the lively soul: and this is the image of the indwelling Spirit.

And these three are one, each equally in itself the whole work, whereof none can exist without other: and this is the image of the Trinity.

DOROTHY L. SAYERS: *The Mind of the Maker*

The real mark of the finitude of the human mind is that no matter what reality it grasps and wrestles with, in some way the reality always escapes. This to me is the real significance of what some people call "the infinite regress," what Kant called "the antinomy," and, fundamentally, what Kierkegaard called "the paradox." The infinite regress, to my mind, is the sign that we are in touch with reality.

I first met the infinite regress when I was a very little boy. We used to eat a breakfast cereal, which I still see in the shops, called Post

Toasties. In those days the box was most fascinating. It contained the picture of a little girl with long hair kneeling in front of a fire. Beside her was a box of Post Toasties, and on that box was a little girl with long hair, beside a fire, and near her was a box of Post Toasties! The artist had given up the ghost quite early, because that third box of Post Toasties had just a little squiggle on it. I was about four or five years old and pointed out to my father that really this never ended, it went on and on, box of Post Toasties, box of Post Toasties, box of Post Toasties, forever. The artist could stop but the philosopher could not! My father replied, "Yes, my boy, but perhaps one day you will think that everything is like that fundamentally." Always, what we are left with is the knowledge that there is more to know. We push on and push on and push on, and we never get to the bottom of reality. The mind of man can never contain all of any reality, not even a box of Post Toasties.

J. V. LANGMEAD CASSERLEY: *Graceful Reason*

In tragedy terrible events occur, we know not why, and ultimately in vain. In comedy terrible events may occur also, but the conclusion shows us why and shows us that they are not in vain. Comedy, properly speaking, must be distinguished from mere farce, as Dante clearly saw when he called his epic description of the whole Christian scheme of destiny *The Divine Comedy*. Tragedy is completely locked up in time and therefore ultimately irrational. Comedy is eschatological and rational, always concerned to show how the end makes sense of all that has come before. We may illustrate by comparing Shakespeare's *Hamlet* with his *A Winter's Tale*. The last act of the written tragedy of *Hamlet* is simply the opening of the unwritten tragedy of young Fortinbras, one finite, temporal episode merely leading to another. *A Winter's Tale* on the other hand concludes with an allegory of resurrection and redemption which makes sense of all that has gone before and shows how all things can be transmuted and made new.

J. V. LANGMEAD CASSERLEY: *Graceful Reason*

Christ proposed the docility of matter to us as a model when he told us to consider the lilies of the field that neither toil nor spin. This means that they have not set out to clothe themselves in this or that color; they have not exercised their will or made arrangements to bring about their object; they have received all that natural necessity brought them. If they appear to be infinitely more beautiful than the richest stuffs, it is not because they are richer but a result of their docility. Materials are docile too, but docile to man, not to God. Matter is not beautiful when it obeys man, but only when it obeys God. If sometimes a work of art seems almost as beautiful as the sea, the mountains, or flowers, it is because the light of God has filled the artist. In order to find things beautiful which are manufactured by men uninspired by God, it would be necessary for us to have understood with our whole soul that these men themselves are only matter, capable of obedience without knowledge. For anyone who has arrived at this point, absolutely everything here below is perfectly beautiful. In everything that exists, in everything that comes about, he discerns the mechanism of necessity, and he appreciates in necessity the infinite sweetness of obedience. For us, this obedience of things in relation to God is what the transparency of a window pane is in relation to light. As soon as we feel this obedience with our whole being, we see God.

SIMONE WEIL: *Waiting for God*

Pied Beauty

Glory be to God for dappled things—
    For skies of couple-color as a brinded cow;
      For rose-moles all in stipple upon trout that swim;
Fresh-firecoal chestnut-falls; finches' wings;
    Landscape plotted and pieced—fold, fallow, and plough;
      And all trades, their gear and tackle and trim.

All things counter, original, spare, strange;
    Whatever is fickle, freckled (who knows how?)
      With swift, slow; sweet, sour; adazzle, dim;
He fathers-forth whose beauty is past change:
        Praise him.

GERARD MANLEY HOPKINS

Time and History

Wonder or radical amazement is the chief characteristic of the religious man's attitude toward history and nature. One attitude is alien to his spirit: taking things for granted, regarding events as a natural course of things. To find an approximate cause of a phenomenon is no answer to his ultimate wonder. He knows that there are laws that regulate the course of natural processes; he is aware of the regularity and pattern of things. However, such knowledge fails to mitigate his sense of perpetual surprise at the fact that there are facts at all. Looking at the world he would say, "This is the Lord's doing, it is marvelous in our eyes" (Psalms 118:23).

That "wonder is the feeling of a philosopher, and philosophy begins in wonder" was stated by Plato and maintained by Aristotle: "For it is owing to their wonder that men both now begin and at first began to philosophize." To this day, rational wonder is appreciated as *"semen scientiae,"* as the seed of knowledge, as something conducive, not indigenous to cognition. Wonder is the prelude to knowledge; it ceases, once the cause of a phenomenon is explained.

But does the worth of wonder merely consist in its being a stimulant to the acquisition of knowledge? Is wonder the same as curiosity? To the prophets wonder is *a form of thinking*. It is not the beginning of knowledge but an act that goes beyond knowledge; it does not come to an end when knowledge is acquired; it is an attitude that never ceases. There is no answer in the world to man's radical amazement.

As civilization advances, the sense of wonder declines. Such decline is an alarming symptom of our state of mind. Mankind will not perish for want of information; but only for want of appreciation. The beginning of our happiness lies in the understanding that life without wonder is not worth living. What we lack is not a will to believe but a will to wonder.

Awareness of the divine begins with wonder. It is the result of what man does with his higher incomprehension. The greatest hindrance to such awareness is our adjustment to conventional notions, to mental clichés. Wonder or radical amazement, the state of maladjustment to words and notions, is therefore a prerequisite for an authentic awareness of that which is.

ABRAHAM J. HESCHEL: *God in Search of Man*

Cant and equivocation dismissed, it seems to me that there are three great bodies of principle and conviction that tie together what is called modern civilization. The first of these is the Christian faith: theological and moral doctrines which inform us, either side of the Atlantic, of the nature of God and man, the fatherhood of God, the brotherhood of man, human dignity, the rights and duties of human persons, the nature of charity, and the meaning of hope and resignation. The second of these is the corpus of imaginative literature, humane letters, which is the essence of our high culture: humanism, which, with Christian faith, teaches us our powers and our limitations —the work of Plato, Virgil, Cicero, Dante, Shakespeare, and so many others. The third is a complex of social and political institutions which we may call the reign of law, or ordered liberty: prescription, precedent, impartial justice, private rights, private property, the character of genuine community, the claims of the family and of voluntary association. However much these three bodies of conviction have been injured by internecine disputes, nihilism, Benthamism, the cult of Rationalism, Marxism, and other modern afflictions, they remain the rocks upon which our civilization is built.

RUSSELL KIRK: "Cultural Debris:
A Mordant Last Word,"
in *The Intemperate Professor*

No life is able to overcome finiteness, sin, and tragedy. The illusions of our period have been that modern civilization *can* conquer them, and that we can achieve security in our own existence. Progress seemed to have conquered tragedy; the divine order seemed to be embodied in the progressive, historical order. But for nearly three decades our generation has received blow after blow, destroying that illusion, and driving to despair and cynicism those who wanted to transform, and thought they could transform, the historical order into a divine order. Let us learn from the catastrophe of our time at least the fact that *no* life and *no* period are able to overcome finiteness, sin, and tragedy.

. . . there is another order to which we, as human beings, belong, an order which makes man *always* dissatisfied with what is given to him. Man transcends everything in the historical order, all the heights and depths of his own existence. He passes, as no other being is able to pass, beyond the limits of his given world. He participates in something infinite, in an order which is not transitory, not self-destructive, not tragic, but eternal, holy, and blessed. Therefore, when he listens to the prophetic word, when he hears of the everlasting God and of the greatness of His power and the mystery of His acts, a response is awakened in the depth of his soul; the infinite within him is touched. Every man knows, in some depths of his soul, that that is true. Our despair itself, our inability to escape ourselves in life and in death, witness to our infinity.

. . . the two orders, the historical and the eternal, although they can never become the same, are within each other. The historical order is not separated from the eternal order. What is new in the prophets and in Christianity, beyond all paganism, old and new, is that the eternal order reveals itself in the historical order. The suffering servant of God and the enemies because of whom He suffers, the Man and the Cross and those who fainted under the Cross, the exiled and persecuted in all periods of history, have all transformed history. The strong in history fall; the strength of each of us is taken from us. But those who seem weak in history finally shape history, because they are bound to the eternal order. We are not a lost generation because we are a suffering, destroyed generation. Each of us belongs to the eternal order, and the prophet speaks to all of us: Comfort ye, comfort ye, my people!

PAUL TILLICH: *The Shaking of the Foundations*

Some ethnologists believe that the whole attempt to derive primitive religions and ethical insights solely from antecedent physical conditions is a grave distortion of the way in which the concepts were formed. Dr. Paul Radin, in his *Primitive Man as Philosopher,* argues that "No progress in ethnology will be achieved until scholars rid themselves once and for all of the curious notion that everything possesses a history; until they realize that certain ideas and certain concepts are as ultimate for man, as a social being, as specific psychological reactions are ultimate for him as a biological being." Among these ideas is the oneness, the truth, the wisdom, and the goodness of God; among them, the concept of His will as the profound law of man's existence; among them, the duty and capacity of man to fulfill or neglect that law and hence to build a human or an inhuman society.

BARBARA WARD: *Faith and Freedom*

In one sense the Jews made the transition we have remarked in other cultures in their times of tribulation—the transition from the idea of an exterior order of ritual law and sacrifice to the idea of an inner righteousness more pleasing to God than the richest material offerings. "Obedience is better than sacrifice and to hearken than the fat of rams." A moral law is perceived in the place of the old ritual law. The Jews, too, believed even more intensely than the Greeks that the disorder in the universe is the inevitable and unalterable consequence of wrongdoing. In their view, man's individual wickedness darkens the world and destroys the harmony of things; moreover, the collective infidelity of the Jewish people is the reason for their disasters and their dispersal. God is a God of righteousness and a God of judgment. The judgments are worked out in time, and if His chosen people dance around the Golden Calf, then sooner or later they will undergo the Babylonian captivity. Disaster is not a sign of God's impotence or of His failure to protect His own people; it is the rod of His anger chastising them for their iniquities. The Assyrian conquerors are the Lord's mysterious instruments in the working out of history, for all things and all peoples are subject to Him and show forth His secret judgments. The Jews as a people may not be aware of this sublime vision. They are as involved as any other nation in the struggle for survival, in wars and disputes and dynastic squabbles, in harvests and in failures of the harvest. It is the great line of Hebrew prophets who interpret to them the meaning of the history in which they are submerged and, like the supreme dramatists of Greece, use the facts of history to illustrate the working out of man's moral destiny.

BARBARA WARD: *Faith and Freedom*

The unique development in Jewish thought was the fashion in which these insights common to all the world religions—of a moral order expressing the will of God for men—were caught up in a vast historical drama unfolding both in time and eternity, involving the entire human race and leading human history to a climax and a conclusion. The starting point is the false choice of the first Adam. Pride and self-love began the alienation of man from God; and matching the physical continuity of the human race, the heredity of genes and chromosomes, there is a spiritual continuity derived from the original moral alienation, a bias away from God and toward the self. Generation after generation, man's wounded nature has involved him in more evil, more self-love, more injustice, and has built up institutions and whole societies mirroring his vanities and his greeds. National pride and economic exploitation—the vitality of the tribe and the vitality of survival—these were the recurrent temptations imbedded in the very fabric of human society and leading in remorseless sequence first to triumph and then to catastrophe.

BARBARA WARD: *Faith and Freedom*

There is one possible explanation which might cover both the uniqueness of Christ's death and resurrection and the resemblances between it and the old fertility cults and mystery religions. It is that they, for all their vague mythology and their frequent degeneration into orgy and delirium, represented a deep and inescapable need in the human heart—a need to express man's dependence and a need to seek eternal aid amid the weariness and evil of Life. When, therefore, in the fullness of time the true God they sought by false roads came to give that strength from beyond nature which they had so anxiously sought, He was born among Jews—the one people who had not compromised with His unique Divinity. But He enacted a drama of sacrifice and triumph of which the archaic rites had been in some sense reflections. Christianity recalls the ancient religions not because it is yet another of them but because it is the original of which they are faint, botched copies.

BARBARA WARD: *Faith and Freedom*

Rationalists of all ages of Western history have regarded the rigorous monotheism of the Hebraic prophets as inferior to this Greek philosophical monism. But they did not observe that the God of the prophets convicted all particular forces in history, including the "elect" nation and its "rulers" and "princes," of violating the divine command of justice while the Greek philosophers were complacent about the social realities of the Greek city-state and lived under the illusion that the rulers were the instruments of justice because they possessed a higher measure of mind. In short, the contingent character of all social achievements was discerned by prophetism and obscured by even the most sophisticated Greek philosophy. The God of the prophets made judgments which left even the elect nation uneasy. The God of Aristotle was a universal mind with which the mind of the philosopher claimed a complacent identity. So the tension between the finite self and the divine self was obscured.

REINHOLD NIEBUHR: *The Self and the Dramas of History*

People who are out to make Christianity look silly go hunting with a double-barrelled gun. If we say that God made the world, they say it is such a rotten place that he has not done a very good job, and that he must be either evil or incompetent. If we say that we always said the world was a fallen world and that we know that there is plenty wrong with it, and the Bible knows that quite as well as they do, they say we are running down human nature and belittling man's achievement. Just let us have a little more knowledge, a little more science, a little more getting together, and everything will be all right in the end. It may be a long time yet, but give man a chance and all will turn out to have been for the best. I cannot for the life of me see why they think so. If they started from God's goodness and thought they knew his plan, there might be some reason for thinking that they could show us how it would all come well in the end. But they do not.

T. R. MILFORD: *Foolishness to the Greeks*

... **the order of history** is an order of sin and punishment. The exile, following the destruction of Jerusalem, was, as all the prophets said, the punishment of the people for their sins. We do not like words such as "sin" and "punishment." They seem to us old-fashioned, barbaric, and invalid in the light of modern psychology. But whenever I have met exiles of high moral standards and insight, I have discovered that they feel responsible for what has happened within their own countries. And very often I have met citizens of democratic countries, citizens of this country, who have expressed a feeling of guilt for the situation in the world today. They were right, and the exiles were right: they are responsible, as are you and I. Whether or not we call it sin, whether or not we call it punishment, we are beaten by the consequences of our own failures. That is the order of history. But at the horizon the other order appears, saying that our struggles are not in vain, that our iniquity is pardoned.

PAUL TILLICH: *The Shaking of the Foundations*

Does religion change? In the realm of the truth that it seeks, never. In the realm of our grasp of the truth, all of the time. The things that are seen are temporary. The things that are unseen, and they alone, are eternal. It was not God who changed, between the Jahvistic legends in the ninth century B.C. and the writing of the latter part of the book of Hosea two or three hundred years later, from a whimsical tyrant to a loving friend. It was man who had grown enough to realize that God must be greater and more gracious than was man himself. It was not essential ethical value that changed when Jesus began to teach. It was Jesus who saw more clearly through fringe to center, through form to meaning, and who thereby changed man's ways of estimating what mattered most. . . .

Let our friends then divest themselves of their first superstition, that religion has not changed since they gave up the particular form of religious expression which they met in their reluctant Sunday School days. Religion has grown at least as much as they have; and religion will help them to grow a great deal more if they will but give heed to the nature of its surging life. Perhaps the major datum for them to learn, at this immediate point, is that the most significant change in religious thinking which has occurred since their childhood has been one of a conscious return to a more authentic and a nobler past. What has occurred in American religious circles has been a vital rediscovery of some of the original emphases of the Hebrew-Christian tradition, and a consequent dropping of many incidentals that derived from sixteenth century Church quarrels and from eighteenth century American isolation. Religion today is in no stage of arrested development. It is high time that the vocal opponents of religion should show cause that the same rightly may be said of them.

GEORGE HEDLEY: *The Superstitions of the Irreligious*

The tradition of religious faith is not a static entity, completed when the Scriptural canon was established, or when the now middle-aged managed at last to escape from regular Sunday School attendance. The concepts of theology are not closed, the structure of an ethical system needs continually to be reexamined in the light of new situations, the experience of worship is something different in community from what it is in solitude. What all this means is that the communion of saints, which produced the riches that this man treasures, has not gone out of business. It still is producing; and if he does not know what its products are today, he is (oh, how this will upset him!) simply out of date.

The religious institutions of our society are by far the oldest social organisms now in existence, much older than the political entities, and having outlived countless changing imperial and national powers, the Church of Jesus Christ carries on today, well into its twentieth successive century, the same work of trying to interpret the issues of life, the same adventure of seeking to solve the riddles of the universe, the same service of inspiration to its people, in which it has engaged from the beginning, and by which it created the values which now our solitary thinks to hug to himself. If, however, he ignores the continuing creativity of the Church, he is clinging to a static revelation rather than sharing in a growing one. It has to be granted that many within the Church do not quite succeed in keeping intellectual and moral pace with the Church's growing discoveries and realizations. It is evident, however, that they have a far better chance to keep up than does he who hears nothing at all of what is going on.

GEORGE HEDLEY: *The Superstitions of the Irreligious*

If, according to Toynbee, the processes in and through which civilizations are born and grow are fundamentally of a religious character, it is equally true that for him the disintegration of a civilization has a profoundly irreligious character. Toynbee describes the disintegration of civilization partly in terms of inertia, of a "resting upon one's oars," a failure on the part of the mature civilization to challenge itself any further from within, and partly in terms of what he calls idolatry—a state of mind in which a society comes to give absolute value to its own being and its own achievements. A disintegrating society is a society that worships itself. The theology of such a worship may be some kind of fanatical nationalism, or a humanism which persuades men to concentrate so entirely upon the values which they know, upon the values which illuminate their own contemporary existence, that they can perceive no other values as transcending them. The values upon which the humanist concentrates may be, and probably are, values indeed, but our values, however valuable, will ruin us if we permit them to blind us to all that lies beyond and above them. Thus, for Toynbee, civilization and its growth is the product of a creative spirituality, whereas its disintegration and decline is the consequence of an exhausted spirituality, in which men make idols of themselves and their own achievements.

J. V. LANGMEAD CASSERLEY: Graceful Reason

... time does not return, nor repeat itself; it runs forward; it is always unique; it ever creates the new. There is within it a drive toward an end, unknown, never to be reached in time itself, always intended and ever fleeing. Time runs toward the "future eternal." This is the greatest of all the mysteries of time. It is the mystery of which the prophets, Christ, and the Apostles have spoken. The eternal is the solution of the riddle of time. Time does not drive toward an endless self-repetition, nor to an empty return to its beginning. Time is not meaningless. It has a hidden meaning—salvation. It has a hidden goal—the Kingdom of God. It brings about a hidden reality—the new creation. The infinite significance of every moment of time is this: in it we decide, and are decided about, with respect to our eternal future.

PAUL TILLICH: The Shaking of the Foundations

If atomic research should by some accident splinter and destroy this whole globe tomorrow, I imagine that it will hurt us no more than that "death on the road" under the menace of which we pass every day of our lives. It will only put an end to a globe which we always knew was doomed to a bad end in any case. I am not sure that it would not be typical of human history if—assuming that the world was bound some day to cease to be a possible habitation for living creatures—men should by their own contrivance hasten that end and anticipate the operation of nature or of time—because it is so much in the character of Divine judgment in history that men are made to execute it upon themselves.

HERBERT BUTTERFIELD: Christianity in History

Knowledge and Education

The fundamental thought underlying nearly everything that we would want to say about the Christian idea of education is that God is the teacher. It is He who establishes all truth; it is He who wills that men shall know the truth; He gives us curious and reflective minds to seek that truth and grasp it and use it; He even gives us the supreme privilege of helping Him in partnership both to teach and to learn. But the initiative is His, just as the truth is His; and all teachers, headmasters, trustees, students, preachers, bishops, and all the rest of the catalog do what they do because God, first of all, does what He does.

STEPHEN F. BAYNE, JR.: "God is the Teacher,"
The Christian Idea of Education

The first thing that a Christian would want to say is that all truth is one. There is only one kind of truth because there is only one God; and you don't have one test for certain aspects of truth and a wholly different one for other aspects. The history the Creed talks about is part and parcel of exactly the same history that Winston Churchill writes about; it is subject to the same tests; it requires the same understanding.

Brotherhood and the table of atomic weights and the Lord's Prayer and the history of the Hittites and the discovery of gunpowder and the Creed and the multiplication table and Heisenberg's principle of uncertainty and the Agnus Dei—all of this and all truth comes to us in one magnificent, tumbling hodge-podge, because it is all God's, and God is one.

STEPHEN F. BAYNE, JR.: "God is the Teacher,"
The Christian Idea of Education

Christianity did not make humanity good, and it cannot be judged by its failure to do so. It is idle to say that Christianity has failed and should therefore be discarded, or to say that it has never been tried. It has been tried, and it hasn't failed. We have failed; but the Christian tradition did not fail to give us and our ancestors everything that could be given to us; and these things—the great ideas which make history intelligible, which made science possible, which established a supernatural justice and mercy as the inescapable standards of judgment by which a society could not help but judge itself—these are what must needs be taught. Indeed they are all that can be taught of Christianity; but they must be taught if western society is to understand itself at all.

STEPHEN F. BAYNE, JR.:
"Understanding Europe from the Inside,"
Schools and Scholarship

What we have to find is a way of seeing the world which shall justify the saint, the artist and the scientist, and give each his full rights. Not a doctrine of watertight compartments, an opposition of appearance to reality. Rather, a doctrine of the indwelling of this visible world by an invisible yet truly existent world of spirit which, while infinitely transcending, yet everywhere supports and permeates the natural scene. Even to say this, is to blur the true issue by resort to the deceptive spatial language which colors and controls our thoughts and translates the dynamic and spiritual into static and intellectual terms.

The first demand we must make of such a diagram is that it shall at least safeguard, though it can never represent, all the best that man has learned to apprehend of the distinct and rich reality of God. . . . For that which above all a genuine theism requires of our human ways of thinking, is the acknowledgement of two sorts or stages of reality, which can never be washed down into one: of a two-foldness that goes right through man's experience and cannot without impoverishment, be resolved. We may call these two sorts of reality, this two-foldness, by various names—Supernature and Nature, Eternity and Time, God and the world, Infinite and finite, Creator and creature. These terms do but emphasize one or another aspect of a total fact too great for us to grasp, without infringing the central truth of its mysterious duality: for God, as Plotinus says, "never was the All. That would make Him dependent on His universe."

EVELYN UNDERHILL: *An Anthology of the Love of God*

It is impossible to look on study, of whatever subject, as of no interest in itself, but only valuable as a means of getting a job. At some points in your studies you are engaged with God's world—the world of nature or the world of man and his mind (though as we have seen, they cannot entirely be separated). God is interested enough in the world to have created it and to sustain it, and to continue to create it. Who are you to despise it? Let us get this clear. There is nothing wrong, there is everything right, in studying to become competent in a profession; in studying engineering in order to be competent to build a bridge; in studying French in order to talk with French people and to understand the French genius and to introduce others to it. There is everything wrong in studying French (or anything else) merely to get a degree and get a living by teaching other people to study French to get a degree . . . bored people teaching bored people boring subjects!

T. R. MILFORD: Foolishness to the Greeks

. . . it is possible for those who have accepted God's word of the cross to find in their work in the university, and particularly in their studies, meaning, point and purpose; and they can do something to redeem the university itself from futility and disintegration. It does not matter much what you are studying. At some point through your mind you are touching God's world. He is interested in it sufficiently to have created it and to keep it in being. Be humble enough to submit yourself to its discipline. All facts are God's facts, and in submitting yourself to them, you submit yourself to him.

I want to say a word to students, particularly those who are beginning their university career. Have faith in God. That means, do not be worried if you do not see the point of everything or how it holds together. We cannot see how it holds together, but it does, because it is God's world. You cannot see, perhaps, how your life is going to be used, nor how your studies will set forward his kingdom. Do not worry; if you are willing, he will make it plain.

Have this mind in you which is also in Christ Jesus—who concentrated on a few people and a limited task, and finished the work that was given him to do. Do not try to be everybody, but get on with your job. If you are capable of it, for God's sake get a first class (for God's sake, of course); and if you can't get that, do as well as you can, for his sake.

T. R. MILFORD: Foolishness to the Greeks

In reading Chesterton, as in reading Macdonald, I did not know what I was letting myself in for. A young man who wishes to remain a sound Atheist cannot be too careful of his reading. There are traps everywhere—"Bibles laid open, millions of surprises," as Herbert says, "fine nets and stratagems." God is, if I may say it, very unscrupulous.

C. S. LEWIS: Surprised by Joy

All the books were beginning to turn against me. Indeed, I must have been as blind as a bat not to have seen, long before, the ludicrous contradiction between my theory of life and my actual experiences as a reader. George Macdonald had done more to me than any other writer; of course it was a pity he had that bee in his bonnet about Christianity. He was good *in spite of it*. Chesterton had more sense than all the other moderns put together; bating, of course, his Christianity. Johnson was one of the few authors whom I felt I could trust utterly; curiously enough, he had the same kink. Spenser and Milton by a strange coincidence had it too. Even among ancient authors the same paradox was to be found. The most religious (Plato, Aeschylus, Virgil) were clearly those on whom I could really feed. On the other hand, those writers who did not suffer from religion and with whom in theory my sympathy ought to have been complete—Shaw and Wells and Mill and Gibbon and Voltaire—all seemed a little thin; what as boys we called "tinny." It wasn't that I didn't like them. They were all (especially Gibbon) entertaining; but hardly more. There seemed to be no depth in them. They were too simple. The roughness and density of life did not appear in their books.

C. S. LEWIS: *Surprised by Joy*

In the field of literature we have been quaintly and destructively inconsistent. It was pretty difficult to leave out Dante Alighieri and John Milton and John Bunyan from the catalogue of major European authors, and so we kept them in at least *pro forma*. There did arise, however, a prevailing judgment that they were pretty boring, and that because they were essentially religious writers. What had happened was that already we had expunged from the curriculum the basic materials which Dante and Milton and Bunyan had used, and so that mostly when we read them we had not the faintest idea what they were talking about. Today the case of T. S. Eliot is creating grave difficulty for secularists who dare not deny his power as a poet, yet who hate his judgment so fiercely that not uncommonly they transfer their hatred to the man. Again one suspects that the real difficulty is that they understand neither the man nor the materials with which he works.

GEORGE HEDLEY: *The Superstitions of the Irreligious*

Judaism perhaps has had better fortune than has Christianity at the point of popular recognition of religious and specifically Biblical scholarship. Learned Rabbis in all the centuries have done remarkable critical work, and their findings have secured appreciably wider dissemination within Judaism than have those of Christian scholars within Christendom. This is particularly true in the United States, where frontier distrust of "eddication" has made life hard for professors in every field, and where popular suspicion of learning has created propaganda alike against braintrusters in Washington and against seminary teachers when they preach in the churches. The Jews, on the other hand, mostly escaped the frontier era in America, and they brought here with them their European respect for the learning of their Rabbinic scholars.

It was an exciting experience for the present writer, and I think for the audience, when recently students in a state college hurled the same Biblical and theological questions at a Rabbi and me, seated side by side on a table at the front of a big lecture room; and when they got from us, time after time, identical answers in the literary and historical fields. The striking thing, however, was that the Rabbi was shocked at the ignorance and naïveté which the students revealed; whereas I, having lived long among Christians, was merely sorry without being surprised.

GEORGE HEDLEY: *The Superstitions of the Irreligious*

The key to a Christian conception of studies is the realization that prayer consists of attention. It is the orientation of all the attention of which the soul is capable toward God. The quality of the attention counts for much in the quality of the prayer. Warmth of heart cannot make up for it.

The highest part of the attention only makes contact with God, when prayer is intense and pure enough for such a contact to be established; but the whole attention is turned toward God.

Of course school exercises only develop a lower kind of attention. Nevertheless, they are extremely effective in increasing the power of attention that will be available at the time of prayer, on condition that they are carried out with a view to this purpose and this purpose alone.

Although people seem to be unaware of it today, the development of the faculty of attention forms the real object and almost the sole interest of studies. Most school tasks have a certain intrinsic interest as well, but such an interest is secondary. All tasks that really call upon the power of attention are interesting for the same reason and to an almost equal degree.

School children and students who love God should never say: "For my part I like mathematics"; "I like French"; "I like Greek." They should learn to like all these subjects, because all of them develop that faculty of attention which, directed toward God, is the very substance of prayer.

SIMONE WEIL: *Wating for God*

The Christian student avoids disintegration, idolatry, and narrowness, when he offers his mind to Christ, so that Christ in his Church may think through him. Does it seem strange that Christ can only think about French or engineering through your mind? At all events, you will agree that he cannot say or write anything except through the mouths and hands of his servants. It is your business to provide him with a well-instructed, competent mind, instead of a feeble and muddly one, strong skillful hands to work with, and a lucid voice to speak. Christians will do more to redeem the world from futility by the conscious dedication of their special skills, in fellowship with one another, and respectful cooperation with all who serve the truth, than by endless discussions of "Christianity and" anything that happens to be hitting the headlines.

T. R. MILFORD: *Foolishness to the Greeks*

Blessed are they that inanimate all their knowledge, consummate all in Christ Jesus. The University is a Paradise, Rivers of knowledge are there, Arts and Sciences flow from thence. Counsel Tables are *Horti conclusi,* (as it is said in the Canticles) *Gardens that are walled in,* and they are *Fontes signati, Wells that are sealed up;* bottomlesse depths of unsearchable Counsels there. But those *Aquae quietudinum,* which the Prophet speaks of, *The waters of rest,* they flow *a magistro bono,* from this good master, and flow into him again; All knowledge that begins not, and ends not with his glory, is but a giddy, but a vertiginous circle, but an elaborate and exquisite ignorance.

JOHN DONNE: *Sermons*

I regard my talent as God-given and I pray to Him daily for the strength to use it. When I discovered that I had been made the custodian of this gift, in my earliest childhood, I pledged myself to God to be worthy of it, but I have received uncovenanted mercies all my life. The custodian has too often kept faith on his all-too-worldly terms.

IGOR STRAVINSKY, on his eightieth birthday:
quoted in the London *Observer*, June 17, 1962

«6» Faith

I now want to say something to agnostics. I do not believe that you or anyone can find the true God just by looking at the universe, and asking, "What is behind it?" But I do say, that if you refuse to consider the possibility of its being made by God for a good purpose, you have a pretty fair problem on your hands. As I said at the beginning, the universe is here, and among other things it has produced us. It contains among other things reasonable beings like you and me (at least let us suppose that we are reasonable), beings capable of love, and unselfish sacrifice, capable of appreciating beauty and creating it, and finding everywhere beauty and order. In fact, the very difficulties we have been considering, the facts of disorder, suffering and evil are difficulties for us only because there is something in us which can stand, as it were, apart from them and say they ought not to be. The problem of evil is only a problem because of the existence of good. The problem of disorder is only a problem when we know what order is. And it seems to me that the agnostic gets away with it too easily. He delights in pointing out the difficulties of believing in God, and stops short of giving any other explanation of the existence of goodness, including beauty and truth. I always find it incredible that Shakespeare and Gandhi, not to mention great examples, have come about by chance; I always find it incredible that order and beauty and heroism come about by accident, and that the mindless movings of innumerable electrons and the rest going on for long enough could, in fact, produce among other things beings who could know them and criticize the electrons and each other. Nor does the magic word of evolution, as understood either by Herbert Spencer or Julian Huxley, explain it.

T. R. MILFORD: *Foolishness to the Greeks*

The law of reversed effort . . . is valid on every level of life, and warns us against the error of making religion too grim and strenuous an affair. Certainly in all life of the spirit the will is active and must retain its conscious and steadfast orientation to God. Heroic activity and moral effort must form an integral part of full human experience. Yet it is clearly possible to make too much of the process of wrestling with evil. An attention chiefly and anxiously concentrated on the struggle with sins and weaknesses, instead of on the eternal sources of happiness and power, will offer the unconscious harmful suggestions of impotence and hence tend to frustration. The early ascetics, who made elaborate preparations for dealing with temptations, got as an inevitable result plenty of temptations with which to deal. A sounder method is taught by the mystics. "When Thoughts of sin press on thee," says *The Cloud of Unknowing,* "look over their shoulders seeking another thing, the which thing is God. . . ."

Give the contemplative faculty its chance, let it breathe for at least a few moments of each day the spiritual atmosphere of faith, hope and love, and the spiritual life will at least in some measure, be realized by it.

EVELYN UNDERHILL: *An Anthology of the Love of God*

Once I heard a man say: "I spent twenty years trying to come to terms with my doubts. Then one day it dawned on me that I had better come to terms with my faith. Now I have passed from the agony of questions I cannot answer into the agony of answers I cannot escape. And it's a great relief."

DAVID E. ROBERTS: *The Grandeur and Misery of Man*

I once heard Dr. Julius Moldenhawer tell of how, when he was a child, he knew so little that he believed the Christmas story, just as St. Luke tells it. Then came a time when he knew so much—after studying higher criticism, comparative religion, and philosophy—that he could not believe the miraculous setting of the story. But now, once again, he knows so little that he believes the story just as St. Luke tells it.

What did he mean? I think he meant that if Christian faith is reached at all, it must be reached through wonder. If we reflect upon it in an ordinary way, we come to the conclusion that Christmas could not possibly happen. By all the rules of common sense, men should long ago have learned what to expect of themselves. They should have reconciled themselves to war, selfishness, and hatred, and have come to terms with these hard facts as best they could. Indeed, so long as we leave God out of account, so long as we focus our attention exclusively upon unredeemed humanity, this picture is perfectly accurate. We can easily see through the pretensions of the so-called "perfectionists." We know that the people who try to act from saintly motives are frequently self-assertive and bad tempered. We have learned by hard experience to be suspicious of those impractical individuals who try to live in terms of pure love. We know how smothering and how intolerant sweet Christians can be. We know the harm well-intentioned visionaries can do. . . .

If Christmas is merely a memory of things past, it cannot heal us. But if it is an awakening to things present, it can be the most healing event ever known. If we can believe that the impossible has happened and that though we have shut Him out, God comes into our world just the same, then a restored humanity and a restored creation may be born again in us today.

DAVID E. ROBERTS: *The Grandeur and Misery of Man*

To my thinking, miracles are never a stumbling-block to the realist. It is not miracles that dispose realists to belief. The genuine realist, if he is an unbeliever, will always find strength and ability to disbelieve in the miraculous, and if he is confronted with a miracle as an irrefutable fact he would rather disbelieve his own senses than admit the fact. Even if he admits it, he admits it as a fact of nature till then unrecognized by him. Faith does not, in the realist, spring from the miracle but the miracle from faith. If the realist once believes, then he is bound by his very realism to admit the miraculous also. The Apostle Thomas said that he would not believe till he saw, but when he did see he said, "My Lord and my God!" Was it the miracle forced him to believe? Most likely not, but he believed solely because he desired to believe and possibly he fully believed in his secret heart, even when he said, "I do not believe till I see."

FYODOR DOSTOYEVSKY: *The Brothers Karamazov*

The best support for faith is the guarantee that if we ask our Father for bread, he does not give us a stone. Quite apart from explicit religious belief, every time that a human being succeeds in making an effort of attention with the sole idea of increasing his grasp of truth, he acquires a greater aptitude for grasping it, even if his effort produces no visible fruit. An Eskimo story explains the origin of light as follows: "In the eternal darkness, the crow, unable to find any food, longed for light, and the earth was illumined." If there is a real desire, if the thing desired is really light, the desire for light produces it. There is a real desire when there is an effort of attention. It is really light that is desired if all other incentives are absent. Even if our efforts of attention seem for years to be producing no result, one day a light that is in exact proportion to them will flood the soul. Every effort adds a little gold to a treasure no power on earth can take away. The useless efforts made by the Curé d'Ars, for long and painful years, in his attempt to learn Latin bore fruit in the marvellous discernment that enabled him to see the very soul of his penitents behind their words and even their silences.

SIMONE WEIL: *Waiting for God*

Christian faith has appeared to many an easy thing; nay, not a few even reckon it among the social virtues, as it were, and this they do because they have not made proof of it experimentally, and have never tasted of what efficacy it is. For it is not possible for any man to write well about it, or to understand well what is rightly written, who has not at some time tasted of its spirit, under the pressure of tribulation; while he who has tasted of it, even to a very small extent, can never write, speak, think, or hear about it sufficiently. For it is a living fountain, springing up unto eternal life, as Christ calls it in John iv.

MARTIN LUTHER: *Concerning Christian Liberty*

Faith is not the human fancy and dream which some people mistake for faith. When such persons see that no amendment of the life and no good works follow, although they may hear and talk much about faith, they fall into error and declare that faith is not enough, but we must perform good works if we would be pious and attain salvation. In consequence of this, when they hear the Gospel, they fall to work and frame for themselves by their own powers a notion in their hearts which says, I believe. This they then consider true faith. But as it is a human invention and notion, of which the heart in its depths finds out nothing, it accomplishes also nothing and no amendment of the life follows.

But faith is a divine work in us, which transforms us and begets us anew from God (John i:13), which crucifies the old Adam, makes us in heart, temper, disposition, and in all our powers entirely different men, and brings with it the Holy Spirit. O, this faith is a living, busy, active, powerful thing! It is impossible that it should not be ceaselessly doing that which is good. It does not even ask whether good works should be done; but before the question can be asked, it has done them, and it is constantly engaged in doing them. But he who does not do such works, is a man without faith. He gropes and casts about him to find faith and good works, not knowing what either of them is, and yet prattles and idly multiplies words about faith and good works.

Faith is a living, well-founded confidence in the grace of God, so perfectly certain that it would die a thousand times rather than surrender its conviction. Such confidence and personal knowledge of divine grace makes its possessor joyful, bold, and full of warm affection toward God and all created things—all of which the Holy Spirit works in faith. Hence, such a man becomes without constraint willing and eager to do good to everyone, to serve everyone, to suffer all manner of ills, in order to please and to glorify God, who has shown toward him such grace. It is thus impossible to separate works from faith—yea, just as impossible as to separate burning and shining from fire. Therefore be on your guard against your own false notions and unprofitable babblings, ye who would be so wise in your opinions about faith and good works, although you are the greatest fools. Pray God that He may work faith in you; otherwise you must remain forever without faith, whatever fancies you may invent and whatever works you may be able to perform.

MARTIN LUTHER: *Preface to St. Paul's*
Epistle to the Romans

If He [God] ask me an idea of my religion and my opinions, shall I not be able to say, It is that which thy word and thy Catholic Church hath imprinted in me? If he ask me an idea of my prayers, shall I not be able to say, It is that which my particular necessities, that which the form prescribed by thy Son, that which the care and piety of the Church in conceiving fit prayers hath imprinted in me? If he ask me an idea of my sermons, shall I not be able to say, It is that which the analogy of faith, the edification of the congregation, the zeal of thy work, the meditations of my heart have imprinted in me?

JOHN DONNE: *Sermons*

. . . **my relationship** to Christianity is no different in its essential from my relationship to physics. In both cases I was moved to respond to a great public body of truth, existing prior to my response to it and continuing after I shall be gone; a public body of truth external to me and standing over against me as an individual Christian or physicist. I do not any more have a faith of my own than I have a physics of my own.

WILLIAM G. POLLARD: *Physicist and Christian*

No, senor. I will not demand of you belief which you can oppose by doubt. I will speak of that which can be pushed from our minds, but cannot be denied. The mystery of our role on earth. The great questions at the beginning and at the end of our existence. Where did we come from? Where do we go? And in between: why are we here? What must we do? What is the meaning and purpose? Questions which cannot be answered with that absolute proof which has become so dear to our hearts. Therefore we push them aside and proceed to live as if they did not surround us on all sides like the very air we breathe. . . . As if the basic mystery did not exist. For man must act and knows not what to do. Imagine a man running and he knows not why or where to. And all the while he thinks, but the answers that would guide him are withheld. And he must make decisions; he must choose directions at the many crossroads of his life, and he knows not his goal. . . . I ask you, senor, can such a man find peace? . . .

But to deny means as little as to proclaim one's faith. Vanities both, no more. For what exists can neither be banished nor flattered by our opinion. The truth is, senor, one way or another we all have to live with our God. Or, if you prefer, with the mystery of our life. How? It is up to each of us. We may choose to evade, to rebel, to ridicule, to hate, to believe. Only one thing is impossible, the very thing most people try—to ignore.

EUGENE VALE: *The Thirteenth Apostle*

On the moment of conversion:

You must picture me alone in that room in Magdalen [Oxford], night after night, feeling, whenever my mind lifted even for a second from my work, the steady, unrelenting approach of Him whom I so earnestly desired not to meet. That which I greatly feared had at last come upon me. In the Trinity Term of 1929 I gave in, and admitted that God was God, and knelt and prayed: perhaps, that night, the most dejected and reluctant convert in all England. I did not then see what is now the most shining and obvious thing; the Divine humility which will accept a convert even on such terms. The Prodigal Son at least walked home on his own feet. But who can duly adore that Love which will open the high gates to a prodigal who is brought in kicking, struggling, resentful, and darting his eyes in every direction for a chance of escape? The words *compelle intrare,* compel them to come in, have been so abused by wicked men that we shudder at them; but, properly understood, they plumb the depth of the Divine mercy. The hardness of God is kinder than the softness of men, and His compulsion is our liberation.

C. S. LEWIS: Surprised by Joy

During the past thirty years people from all the civilized countries of the earth have consulted me. . . . Among all my patients in the second half of life—that is to say over thirty-five—there has not been one whose problem in the last resort was not that of finding a religious outlook on life. It is safe to say that every one of them fell ill because he had lost that which the living religions of every age have given to their followers, and none of them has been really healed who did not regain his religious outlook.

C. S. YOUNG: quoted in The Listener, April 23, 1953

The thing I am here to say to you is this: that it is worse than useless for Christians to talk about the importance of Christian morality, unless they are prepared to take their stand upon the fundamentals of Christian theology. It is a lie to say that dogma does not matter; it matters enormously. It is fatal to let people suppose that Christianity is only a mode of feeling; it is vitally necessary to insist that it is first and foremost a rational explanation of the universe. It is hopeless to offer

Christianity as a vaguely idealistic aspiration of a simple and consoling kind; it is, on the contrary, a hard, tough, exacting, and complex doctrine, steeped in a drastic and uncompromising realism. And it is fatal to imagine that everybody knows quite well what Christianity is and needs only a little encouragement to practise it. The brutal fact is that in this Christian country not one person in a hundred has the faintest notion what the Church teaches about God or man or society or the person of Jesus Christ.

DOROTHY L. SAYERS: *Creed or Chaos*

Humanity needs rocklike men—men appointed once for all. It needs to know that, in the flux of the world, there still exist enduring islets of absolute fidelity and affirmation. The greatest service at the present time that one can render to the human race is to affirm the absolute. The negation of the absolute is the great modern malady. Humanity needs to know that there are men who do not disappear.

LE FRÈRE UNTEL (JEAN-PAUL DESBIENS):
Letter to a Young Brother

One can say without fear of exaggeration that today the spirit of truth is almost absent from religious life.

This is observable among other things in the nature of the arguments adduced in favor of Christianity. Many of them are of the publicity type associated with "pink pills." It is the case with Bergson and all that draws its inspiration from him. In Bergson, religious faith appears after the manner of a "pink pill" of a superior kind, which imparts an astonishing amount of vitality. The same thing applies to the historical argument, which runs in this sort, "Look what a miserable lot men were before Christ. Christ came, and see how men, in spite of their backslidings, afterward became, on the whole a good lot!" That is absolutely contrary to the truth. But even if it were true, it reduced apologetics to the level of advertisements for pharmaceutical products, which describe the state of the patient before and after. It is measuring the effectiveness of Christ's Passion, which, if it is not fictitious, is necessarily infinite, by an historical, temporal, and human result, which, even if it were real, which it isn't, would necessarily be finite.

Pragmatism has encroached upon and profaned the very conception of faith.

SIMONE WEIL: The Need for Roots

Socrates was wont to say, They are most happy and nearest the gods that needed nothing. And coming once up into the Exchange at Athens, where they that traded, asked him, What will you buy? What do you lack?, after he had gravely walked up into the middle, spreading forth his hands and turning about: Good gods, said he, who would have thought there were so many things in the world which I do not want?—and so left the place under the reproach of Nature. He was wont to say That happiness consisted not in having many, but in needing the fewest things. . . . We need heaven and earth, our senses, souls, and bodies to be enjoyed. Which, God of his mercy having freely prepared, they are most happy that so live in the enjoyment of these, as to need no accidental, trivial things, no splendors, pomps and vanities.

THOMAS TRAHERNE: Centuries of Meditations

Faith is a state of the mind and the soul. In this sense we can understand the words of the Spanish mystic St. John of the Cross: "Faith is the union of God with the soul." The language of religion is a set of formulas which register a basic spiritual experience. It must not be regarded as describing, in terms to be defined by philosophy, the reality which is accessible to our senses and which we can analyse with the tools of logic. I was late in understanding what this meant. When I finally reached that point, the beliefs in which I was once brought up and which, in fact, had given my life direction even while my intellect still challenged their validity, were recognized by me as mine in their own right, and by my free choice. I feel that I can endorse those convictions without any compromise with the demands of that intellectual honesty which is the very key to maturity of mind.

DAG HAMMARKSJÖLD: writing in British Weekly

We act in faith—and miracles occur. In consequence, we are tempted to make the miracles the ground for our faith. The cost of such weakness is that we lose the confidence of faith. Faith *is,* faith creates, faith

carries. It is not derived from, nor created, nor carried by anything
except its own reality.

DAG HAMMARSKJÖLD: Markings

The Universal Church is today, it seems to me, more definitely set
against the World than at any time since pagan Rome. I do not mean
that our times are particularly corrupt; all times are corrupt. I mean
that Christianity, in spite of certain local appearances, is not, and cannot be within measurable time, "official." The World is trying the
experiment of attempting to form a civilized but non-Christian men-
tality. The experiment will fail; but we must be very patient in awaiting
its collapse; meanwhile redeeming the time: so that the Faith may be
preserved alive through the dark ages before us; to renew and rebuild
civilization, and save the World from suicide.

T. S. ELIOT: "Thoughts After Lambeth," Selected Essays

Prayer

Be not afraid to pray—to pray is right.
Pray, if thou canst, with hope; but ever pray,
Though hope be weak, or sick with long delay;
Pray in the darkness, if there be no light.
Far is the time, remote from human sight,
When war and discord on the earth shall cease;
Yet every prayer for universal peace
Avails the blessed time to expedite.
Whate'er is good to wish, ask that of Heaven,
Though it be what thou canst not hope to see;
Pray to be perfect, though material leaven
Forbid the spirit so on earth to be:
    But if for any wish thou darest not to pray,
    Then pray to God to cast that wish away.

HARTLEY COLERIDGE

We call prayer in the pregnant sense of the term that speech of man
to God which, whatever else is asked, ultimately asks for the manifes-

tation of the divine Presence, for this Presence's becoming dialogically perceivable. The single presupposition of a genuine state of prayer is thus the readiness of the whole man for this Presence, simple turned-towardness, unreserved spontaneity. This spontaneity, ascending from the roots, succeeds time and again in overcoming all that disturbs and diverts. But in this our stage of subjectivized reflection not only the concentration of the one who prays, but also his spontaneity is assailed. The assailant is consciousness, the over-consciousness of this man here that he is praying, that he is *praying,* that *he* is praying. And the assailant appears to be invincible. The subjective knowledge of the one turning-towards about his turning-towards, this holding back of an I to which the action is an object—all this depossesses the moment, takes away its spontaneity. The specifically modern man who has not yet let go of God knows what that means: he who is not present perceives no Presence.

MARTIN BUBER: *Eclipse of God*

There are, no doubt, passages in the New Testament which may seem at first sight to promise an invariable granting of our prayers. But that cannot be what they really mean. For in the very heart of the story we meet a glaring instance to the contrary. In Gethsemane the holiest of all petitioners prayed three times that a certain cup might pass from Him. It did not. After that the idea that prayer is recommended to us as a sort of infallible gimmick may be dismissed. . . . It would be even worse to think of those who get what they pray for as a sort of court favorites, people who have influence with the throne. The refused prayer of Christ in Gethsemane is answer enough to that. And I dare not leave out the hard saying which I once heard from an experienced Christian: "I have seen many striking answers to prayer and more than one that I thought miraculous. But they usually come at the beginning: before conversion, or soon after it. As the Christian life proceeds, they tend to be rarer. The refusals, too, are not only more frequent; they become more unmistakable, more emphatic."

C. S. LEWIS: *The World's Last Night*

Do not entertain the notion that you ought to *advance* in your prayer. If you do, you will only find you have put on the brake instead of the accelerator. All real progress in spiritual things comes gently, imperceptibly, and is the work of God. Our crude efforts spoil it. Know yourself for the childish, limited and dependent soul you are. Remember that only growth which matters happens without our knowledge and that trying to stretch ourselves is both dangerous and silly. Think of the Infinite Goodness, never of your own taste. Realize that the very capacity to pray at all is the free gift of the Divine Love and be content with St. Francis de Sales' favorite prayer in which all personal religion is summed up. "Yes, Father! Yes, and always Yes!". . .

Let us rejoice in the great adoring acts and splendid heroisms of God's great lovers and humbly do the little bit we can. We too have our place.

EVELYN UNDERHILL: *An Anthology of the Love of God*

Until last September I had never once prayed in all my life, at least not in the literal sense of the word. I had never said any words to God, either out loud or mentally. I had never pronounced a liturgical prayer. I had occasionally recited the *Salve Regina,* but only as a beautiful poem.

Last summer, doing Greek with T——, I went through the Our Father word for word in Greek. We promised each other to learn it by heart. I do not think he ever did so, but some weeks later, as I was turning over the pages of the Gospel, I said to myself that since I had promised to do this thing and it was good, I ought to do it. I did it. The infinite sweetness of this Greek text so took hold of me that for several days I could not stop myself from saying it over all the time. A week afterward I began the vine harvest. I recited the Our Father in Greek every day before work, and I repeated it very often in the vineyard.

Since that time I have made a practice of saying it through once each morning with absolute attention. If during the recitation my attention wanders or goes to sleep, in the minutest degree, I begin again until I have once succeeded in going through it with absolutely pure attention. Sometimes it comes about that I say it again out of sheer pleasure, but I only do it if I really feel the impulse.

The effect of this practice is extraordinary and surprises me every time, for, although I experience it each day, it exceeds my expectation at each repetition.

At times the very first words tear my thoughts from my body and transport it to a place outside space where there is neither perspective nor point of view. The infinity of the ordinary expanses of perception is replaced by an infinity to the second or sometimes the third degree. At the same time, filling every part of this infinity of infinity, there is silence, a silence which is not an absence of sound but which is the object of a positive sensation, more positive than that of sound. Noises, if there are any, only reach me after crossing this silence.

Sometimes, also, during this recitation or at other moments, Christ is present with me in person, but his presence is infinitely more real, more moving, more clear than on that first occasion when he took possession of me.

I should never have been able to take it upon myself to tell you all this had it not been for the fact that I am going away. And as I am going more or less with the idea of probable death, I do not believe that I have the right to keep it to myself. It concerns God, I am really nothing in it at all. If one could imagine any possibility of error in God, I should think that it had all happened to me by mistake. But perhaps God likes to use castaway objects, waste, rejects. After all, should the bread of the host be moldy, it would become the Body of Christ just the same after the priest had consecrated it. Only it cannot refuse, while we can disobey. It sometimes seems to me that when I am treated in so merciful a way, every sin on my part must be a mortal sin. And I am constantly committing them. . . .

First you once said to me at the beginning of our relationship some words that went to the bottom of my soul. You said: "Be very careful, because if you should pass over something important through your own fault it would be a pity."

That made me see intellectual honesty in a new light. Till then I had only thought of it as opposed to faith; your words made me think that perhaps, without my knowing it, there were in me obstacles to the faith, impure obstacles, such as prejudices, habits. I felt that after having said to myself for so many years simply: "Perhaps all that is not true," I ought, without ceasing to say it—I still take care to say it very often now—to join it to the opposite formula, namely: "Perhaps all that is true," and to make them alternate.

SIMONE WEIL: *Waiting for God*

The Our Father contains all possible petitions; we cannot conceive of any prayer not already contained in it. It is to prayer what Christ is to humanity. It is impossible to say it once through, giving the fullest possible attention to each word, without a change, infinitesimal perhaps but real, taking place in the soul.

SIMONE WEIL: *Waiting for God*

But when we consider with a religious seriousness, the manifold weaknesses of the strongest devotions in time of Prayer, it is a sad consideration. I throw my selfe downe in my Chamber, and I call in, and invite God, and his Angels thither, and when they are there, I neglect God and his Angels, for the noise of a Flie, for the ratling of a Coach, for the whining of a doore; I talke on, in the same posture of praying; Eyes lifted up; knees bowed downe; as though I prayed to God; and, if God, or his Angels should ask me, when I thought last of God in that prayer, I cannot tell. A memory of yesterdays pleasures, a feare of to morrows dangers, a straw under my knee, a noise in mine eare, a light in mine eye, an any thing, a nothing, a fancy, a Chimera in my braine, troubles me in my prayer. So certainely is there nothing, nothing in spirituall things, perfect in this world.

JOHN DONNE: *Sermons*

That soule, that is accustomed to direct her selfe to God, upon every occasion, that, as a flowre at Sun-rising, conceives a sense of God, in every beame of his, and spreads and dilates it selfe towards him, in a thankfulnesse, in every small blessing that he sheds upon her; that soule, that as a flowre at the Suns declining, contracts and gathers in, and shuts up her selfe, as though she had received a blow, when soever she heares her Saviour wounded by a oath, or blasphemy, or execration; that soule, who, whatsoever string be strucken in her base or treble, her high or her low estate, is ever tun'd toward God, that soule prayes sometimes when it does not know that it prayes.

JOHN DONNE: *Sermons*

Love

Pure Love or Charity—utter self-giving which is our reply to the Love of God—is the same as sanctity. What is pure love? That which gives and gives and never demands. In the words of Gertrude More: *Courageous, humble, constant: not worn out with labors, not daunted by difficulties*—bravely sticking it out when tired, disheartened, worried. And to do this, we look beyond it all, trying to respond to the Love of God, seeking and serving Christ in our fellow-men. If we do that faithfully, give ourselves to God's purposes, we will develop such depth of peaceful devoted love as passes beyond the need of being fed by feeling or the consolations of religion—the chocolate creams of the Christian life. Do not make the mistake of thinking if you feel cold and dead, that you do not know how to love.

EVELYN UNDERHILL: *An Anthology of the Love of God*

"The fruit of the Spirit," says St. Paul, "is Love, Joy, Peace, Long-Suffering, Gentleness, Goodness, Faithfulness, Meekness, Temperance"—all the things the world most needs. . . . I do not think St. Paul arranged his list of the fruits of the Spirit in a casual order. They represent a progressive series from one point, and that one point is Love, the living, eternal seed from which all grow. We all know that Christians are baptized "into a life summed up in love," even though we have to spend the rest of our own lives learning how to do it. Love, therefore, is the budding-point from which all the rest come: that tender, cherishing attitude; that unlimited self-forgetfulness, generosity and kindness which is the attitude of God to all His creatures; and so must be the attitude towards them which His Spirit brings forth in us. . . . To be unloving is to be out of touch with God. So the generous, cherishing Divine Love, the indiscriminate delight in others, just or unjust, must be our model too. To come down to brass tacks, God loves the horrid man at the fish shop, and the tiresome woman in the next flat, and the disappointing Vicar . . . and the contractor who has cut down the row of trees we loved, to build a row of revolting bungalows. God loves, not tolerates, these wayward, half-grown, self-centered spirits, and seeks without ceasing to draw them into His love. And the first-fruit of His indwelling presence, the first sign that we are on His side and He on ours, must be at least a tiny bud of this Charity breaking the hard and rigid outline of life. . . .

Only Love, Charity, in its deep peacefulness and abiding joy, can embrace all human inconsistency and imperfection and see within it the stirring of the Perfect. But so God loves the world. Not its more spiritual inhabitants. Not its church-wardens and sacristans and pious old ladies—but the world.

EVELYN UNDERHILL: *An Anthology of the Love of God*

"Love one another, Fathers," said Father Zossima, as far as Alyosha could remember afterwards. "Love God's people. Because we have come here and shut ourselves within these walls, we are no holier than those that are outside, but on the contrary, from the very fact of coming here, each of us has confessed to himself that he is worse than others, than all men on earth. . . . And the longer the monk lives in his seclusion, the more keenly he must recognise that. Else he would have no reason to come here. When he realises that he is not only worse than others, but that he is responsible to all men for all and everything, for all human sins, national and individual, only then the aim of our seclusion is attained. For know, dear ones, that every one of us is undoubtedly responsible for all men and everything on earth, not merely through the general sinfulness of creation, but each one personally for all mankind and every individual man. This knowledge is the crown of life for the monk and for every man. For monks are not a special sort of men, but only what all men ought to be. Only through that knowledge, our heart grows soft with infinite, universal, inexhaustible love. Then every one of you will have the power to win over the whole world by love and to wash away the sins of the world with your tears. . . . Each of you keep watch over your heart and confess your sins to yourself unceasingly. Be not afraid of your sins, even when perceiving them, if only there be penitence, but make no conditions with God. Again I say, Be not proud. Be proud neither to the little nor to the great. Hate not those who reject you, who insult you, who abuse and slander you. Hate not the atheists, the teachers of evil, the materialists—and I mean not only the good ones—for there are many good ones among them, especially in our day—hate not even the wicked ones. Remember them in your prayers thus: Save, O Lord, all those who have none to pray for them, save too all those who will not pray. And add: it is not in pride that I make this prayer, O Lord, for I am lower than all men. . . . Love God's people, let not strangers draw away from the flock, for if you slumber in your slothfulness and disdainful pride, or worse still, in covetousness, they will come from all sides and draw away your flock. Expound the Gospel to the people unceasingly . . . be not extortionate. . . . Do not love gold and silver, do not hoard them. . . . Have faith. Cling to the banner and raise it on high."

FYODOR DOSTOYEVSKY: *The Brothers Karamazov*

Brothers, have no fear of men's sin. Love a man even in his sin, for that is the semblance of Divine Love and is the highest love on earth. Love all God's creation, the whole and every grain of sand in it. Love every leaf, every ray of God's light. Love the animals, love the plants, love everything. If you love everything, you will perceive the divine mystery in things. Once you perceive it, you will begin to comprehend it better every day. And you will come at last to love the whole world with an all-embracing love. Love the animals: God has given them the rudiments of thought and joy untroubled. Do not trouble it, don't harass them, don't deprive them of their happiness, don't work against God's intent. Man, do not pride yourself on superiority to the animals; they are without sin, and you, with your greatness, defile the earth by your appearance on it, and leave the traces of your foulness after you—alas, it is true of almost every one of us! Love children especially, for they too are sinless like the angels: they live to soften and purify our hearts and as it were to guide us. Woe to him who offends a child!

FYODOR DOSTOYEVSKY: *The Brothers Karamazov*

You asked for a loving God: you have one. The great spirit you so lightly invoked, the "lord of terrible aspect," is present: not a senile benevolence that drowsily wishes you to be happy in your own way, not the cold philanthropy of a conscientious magistrate, nor the care of a host who feels responsible for the comfort of his guests, but the consuming fire Himself, the Love that made the worlds, persistent as the artist's love for his work and despotic as a man's love for a dog, provident and venerable as a father's love for a child, jealous, inexorable, exacting as love between sexes.

C. S. LEWIS: *The Problem of Pain*

The love of our neighbor is the love which comes down from God to man. It precedes that which rises from men to God. God is longing to come down to those in affliction. As soon as a soul is disposed to consent, though it were the last, the most miserable, the most deformed of souls, God will precipitate himself into it in order, through it, to look at and listen to the afflicted. Only as time passes does the soul become aware that he is there. But, though it finds no name for him, wherever the afflicted are loved for themselves alone, it is God who is present.

God is not present, even if we invoke him, where the afflicted are merely regarded as an occasion for doing good. They may even be loved on this account, but then they are in their natural role, the role of matter and of things. We have to bring to them in their inert, anonymous condition a personal love.

SIMONE WEIL: *Waiting for God*

There are certain things that our age needs, and certain things it should avoid. It needs compassion and a wish that mankind should be happy: it needs the desire for knowledge and the determination to eschew pleasant myths; it needs, above all, courageous hope and the impulse to creativeness. . . . The root of the matter is a very simple and old-fashioned thing, a thing so simple that I am almost ashamed to mention it for fear of the derisive smile with which wise cynics will greet my words. The thing I mean—please forgive me for mentioning it—is love, Christian love, or compassion. If you feel this, you have a motive for existence, a guide in action, a reason for courage, an imperative necessity for intellectual honesty.

BERTRAND RUSSELL: *Impact of Science on Society*

A condition of such love is that it should not be balanced against some system of exact rewards or punishments. Love which knows that every demonstration will open the cupboard door would quickly degenerate into self-interest. The fact that the wicked flourish like the green bay tree has always been a scandal to the would-be just. No poet has expressed the agony more keenly than Gerard Manley Hopkins:

> Wert thou my enemy, O thou my friend,
> How wouldst thou worse, I wonder, than thou dost
> Defeat, thwart me? Oh the sots and thralls of lust

Do in spare hours more thrive than I that spend
Sir, life upon thy cause.

Yet consider the opposite—a universe in which every virtuous act were followed by earthly success and every aspiration toward the good—which is the essence of the love of God—were instantly rewarded with mental ease and physical comfort. Under such conditions how soon would a selfish calculus of advantage stifle that pure disinterested search for the good which is the crown of every moral being, that spendthrift love which repays neglect and indifference with devotion and fills up. with its own full measure the inadequacy of another's response, the love, one should remark, most prized by the world's greatest creator, Shakespeare, the love of Imogen, the love of Cordelia, the love of the dying Desdemona? It seems as though the very disharmonies and injustices of the universe are a condition of producing its supremest good. As the great nineteenth-century liberal Walter Bagehot wrote: "We could not be what we ought to be, if we lived in the sort of universe we should expect . . . a latent Providence, a confused life, an odd material world, our existence broken short in the midst are not real difficulties but real helps . . . they, or something like them, are essential conditions of a moral life in a subordinate being."

BARBARA WARD: *Faith and Freedom*

Love bade me welcome: yet my soul drew back,
    Guiltie of lust and sinne.
But quick-ey'd Love, observing me grow slack
    From my first entrance in,
Drew nearer to me, sweetly questioning,
    If I lack'd any thing.

A guest, I answer'd, worthy to be here:
    Love said, You shall be he.
I the unkinde, ungratefull? Ah my deare,
    I cannot look on thee.
Love took my hand, and smiling did reply,
    Who made the eyes but I?

Truth Lord, but I have marr'd them: let my shame
    Go where it doth deserve.
And know you not, sayes Love, who bore the blame?
    My deare, then I will serve.
You must sit down, sayes Love, and taste my meat:
    So I did sit and eat.

GEORGE HERBERT

Saints

True sanctity does not consist in trying to live without creatures. It consists in using the goods of life in order to do the will of God. It consists in using God's creation in such a way that everything we touch and see and use and love gives new glory to God. To be a saint means to pass through the world gathering fruits for heaven from every tree and reaping God's glory in every field. The saint is one who is in contact with God in every possible way, in every possible direction. He is united to God in the depths of his own being. He sees and touches God in everything and everyone around him. Everywhere he goes, the world rings and resounds (though silently) with the deep pure harmonies of God's glory.

THOMAS MERTON: Seasons of Celebration

God has never given Himself, and never will, to a will alien to His own; where He finds His will, He gives Himself.

MEISTER ECKHART

Joy is peace for having done that which we ought to have done. . . . To have something to doe, to doe it, and then to Rejoice in having done it, to embrace a calling, to performe the Duties of that calling, to joy and rest in the peaceful testimony of having done so; this is Christianly done, Christ did it; Angelically done, Angels doe it; Godly done, God does it.

JOHN DONNE: Sermons

We all know what help it is to live amongst and be intimate with, keen Christians; how much we owe in our lives to contact with them and how hard it is to struggle on alone in a preponderantly non-Christian atmosphere. In the saints we always have the bracing society of keen Christians. We are always in touch with the classic standard. Their personal influence still radiates, centuries after they have left the earth, reminding us of the infinite variety of ways in which the Spirit of God acts on men through men, and reminding us, too, of our own awful responsibility in this matter. The saints are the great experimental Christians, who, because of their unreserved self-dedication have made the great discoveries about God; and as we read their lives and works they will impart to us just so much of these discoveries as we are able to bear. Indeed, as we grow more and more, the saints tell us more and more: disclosing at each fresh reading secrets we did not suspect. Their books are the work of specialists from whom we can humbly learn more of God and our own souls.

EVELYN UNDERHILL: *An Anthology of the Love of God*

We do not think of a martyr simply as a good Christian who has been killed, because he is a Christian: for that would be solely to mourn. We do not think of him simply as a good Christian who has been elevated to the company of the Saints: for that would be simply to rejoice: and neither our mourning nor our rejoicing is as the world's is. A Christian martyrdom is no accident. Saints are not made by accident. Still less is a Christian martyrdom the effect of a man's will to become a ruler of men. Ambition fortifies the will of a man to become ruler over other men: it operates with deception, cajolerie, and violence, it is the action of impurity upon impurity. Not so in Heaven. A martyr, a saint, is always made by the design of God, for his love of men, to warn them and to lead them, to bring them back to his ways. A martyrdom is never the design of man, for the true martyr is he who has become the instrument of God, who has lost his will in the will of God; not lost it, but found it, for he has found freedom in submission to God. The martyr no longer desires anything for himself, not even the glory of martyrdom. . . . So in Heaven the Saints are most high, having made themselves most low.

T. S. ELIOT: *Murder in the Cathedral*

Good and evil we know in the field of this world grow up together almost inseparable. . . . He that can apprehend and consider vice with all her baits and seeming pleasures, and yet abstain, and yet distinguish and yet prefer that which is truly better, he is the true warfaring Christian. I cannot praise a fugitive and cloistered virtue, unexercised and unbreathed, that never sallies out and sees her adversary, but slinks out of the race, where that immortal garland is to be run for not without dust and heat. Assuredly we bring not innocence into the world, we bring impurity much rather: that which purifies us is trial, and trial is by what is contrary. . . .

If every action, which is good or evil in man at ripe years, were to be under pittance and prescription and compulsion, what were virtue but a name, what praise would then be due to well-doing? . . . Many there be that complain of Divine Providence for suffering Adam to transgress; foolish tongues! When God gave him reason, He gave him freedom to choose, for reason is but choosing. . . . We ourselves esteem not of that obedience or love, or gift, which is of force: God therefore left him free, set before him a provoking object, ever almost in his eyes; herein consisted his merit, herein the right of his reward, the praise of his abstinence. Wherefore did He create passions within us, pleasures round about us, but that these rightly tempered are the very ingredients of virtue?

JOHN MILTON: *Areopagitica*

It is true that behind all these quackeries there is a certain body of genuine scientific physiology. But was there any the less a certain body of genuine psychology behind St. Catherine and the Holy Ghost? And which is the healthier mind? that saintly mind or the monkey gland mind?

GEORGE BERNARD SHAW: Preface to *Saint Joan*

Now you know. When the worries over your work loosen their grip, then this experience of light, warmth, and power. From without—a sustaining element, like air to the glider or water to the swimmer. An intellectual hesitation which demands proofs and logical demonstration prevents me from "believing"—in this, too. Prevents me from expressing and interpreting this reality in intellectual terms. Yet, through me there flashes this vision of a magnetic field in the soul, created in a timeless present by unknown multitudes, living in holy obedience, whose words and actions are a timeless prayer.

—"The Communion of Saints"—and—within it—an eternal life.

DAG HAMMARSKJÖLD: *Markings*

In our era, the road to holiness necessarily passes through the world of action.

DAG HAMMARSKJÖLD: *Markings*

. . . no true prophet has ever prophesied voluntarily. It has been forced upon him by a Divine Voice to which he has not been able to close his ears.

PAUL TILLICH: *The Shaking of the Foundations*

O God, that madest this beautiful earth, when will it be ready to receive Thy saints? How long, O Lord, how long?

GEORGE BERNARD SHAW: *Saint Joan*

Worship

Of course, it is possible to worship God on the mountain top. It is possible to worship God also on the polo field, or driving along the highway, or in a baseball park. It is likely that God has been truly worshipped in all of these places. If, however, we raise the question of statistical probability, we scarcely shall maintain that the worship of God is quite as frequent there as it is in the houses built in his honor and devoted to his praise. I have told elsewhere the story of the father who said, "Come on, we can sing hymns on the beach," to whom the little girl replied, "But we won't, will we?" We can. But do we?

It is just a little difficult to be polite about this popular way of trying to justify non-attendance at services of worship. I suggest that it is a reasonable supposition that the people who go to church get quite as much out of the worship of God in nature as do those whose temple is the forest only. In point of fact the nature-is-enough approach is likely to be utterly sentimental, without either the moral content or the personal consecration that are essential to worship rightly so called. This is why Wordsworth is so inferior to the ancient Psalmists. He, as they, saw God in the starry heavens above; but they were the ones who knew this God to be present also in the moral law. Much current worship of "God in nature" is nothing more than an unreflective and unmoral pantheism; and it will not be corrected until the God of physical nature is met also among those other creations of his whom we know as men and women.

GEORGE HEDLEY: *The Superstitions of the Irreligious*

The virtue of religious practices is due to a contact with what is perfectly pure, resulting in the destruction of evil. Nothing here below is perfectly pure except the total beauty of the universe, and that we are unable to feel directly until we are very far advanced in the way of perfection. Moreover, this total beauty cannot be contained in anything tangible, though it is itself tangible in a certain sense.

Religious things are special tangible things, existing here below and yet perfectly pure. This is not on account of their own particular character. The church may be ugly, the singing out of tune, the priest corrupt, and the faithful inattentive. In a sense that is of no importance. It is as with a geometrician who draws a figure to illustrate a proof. If the lines are not straight and the circles are not round it is of no importance. Religious things are pure by right, theoretically, hypothetically, by convention. Therefore their purity is unconditioned. No stain can sully it. That is why it is perfect. It is not, however, perfect in the same way as Roland's mare, which, while it had all possible virtues, had also the drawback of not existing. Human conventions are useless if they are not connected with motives that impel people to observe them. In themselves they are simple abstractions; they are unreal and have no effect. But the convention by which religious things are pure is ratified by God himself. Thus it is an effective convention, a convention containing virtue and operating of itself. This purity is unconditioned and perfect, and at the same time real.

SIMONE WEIL: *Waiting for God*

The source of humility is the habit of realizing the presence of God. Humility does not mean thinking less of yourself than of other people, nor does it mean having a low opinion of your own gifts. It means freedom from thinking about yourself one way or the other at all. It may be quite right that a man conscious of certain powers given him by God should desire the opportunity to exercise these powers for God. It may be quite right that under certain circumstances a man should insist that he is more capable than another man of doing something that must be done. No one would select as an example of humility the elder Pitt; but there was nothing contrary to humility in his alleged declaration to the Duke of Devonshire: "I know that I can save this country and I know that no one else can." He knew the political life of the time pretty well; he was conscious of power in himself; only if he set about his task in his own interest or for self-glorification did he fail in humility.

Humility means that you feel yourself, as a distinct person, out of count, and give your whole mind and thought to the object towards which they are directed, to God himself in worship and to the fulfillment of His will in Christian love; and humility, in that sense, is quite plainly a source of effectiveness. The humility which consists in being a great deal occupied about yourself, and saying you are of little worth, is not Christian humility. It is one form of self-occupation and a very poor and futile one at that; but real humility makes for effectiveness because it delivers a man from anxiety, and we all know that in all undertakings, from the smallest to the greatest, the chief source of feebleness is anxiety. Even in a game we all know that nothing so much paralyses good play as anxiety. If you once begin to wonder whether you are going to catch the ball you will drop it, but if you just catch it without thinking about anything but catching it—not above all, of what other people are going to think of you—probably you will hold it. That goes through everything from such a simple act to the greatest. But there is nothing big enough to hold a man's soul in detachment from the center of himself through all the occupations of life except the majesty of God and His love; and it is in worship, worship given to God because He is God, that man will most learn the secret of real humility.

WILLIAM TEMPLE: *Christ in His Church*

We praise Thee, O God, for Thy glory displayed in all the creatures of
  the earth,

In the snow, in the rain, in the wind, in the storm; in all of Thy creatures,
 both the hunters and the hunted. . . .
They affirm Thee in living; all things affirm Thee in living; the bird in
 the air, both the hawk and the finch; the beast on the earth, both the
 wolf and the lamb; the worm in the soil and the worm in the belly.
Therefore man, whom Thou hast made to be conscious of Thee, must
 consciously praise Thee, in thought and in word and deed.
Even with the hand to the broom, the back bent in laying the fire, the
 knee bent in cleaning the hearth . . .
The back bent under toil, the knee bent under sin, the hands bent to
 the face under fear, the head bent under grief,
Even in us the voices of seasons, the snuffle of winter, the song of spring,
 the drone of summer, the voices of beasts and of birds, praise Thee.

T. S. ELIOT: *Murder in the Cathedral*

Late have I loved Thee, O Beauty so ancient and so new; late
have I loved Thee! For behold Thou were within me, and I outside; and
I thought Thee outside and in my unloveliness fell upon those lovely
things that Thou hast made. Thou wert with me and I was not with
Thee. I was kept from Thee by those things, yet had they not been in
Thee, they would not have been at all. Thou didst call and cry to me
and break open my deafness: and Thou didst send forth Thy beams and
shine upon me and chase away my blindness: Thou didst breathe frag-
rance upon me, and I drew in my breath and do now pant for Thee. I
tasted Thee, and now hunger and thirst for Thee: Thou didst touch me,
and I have burned for Thy peace.

ST. AUGUSTINE: *Confessions*

To worship is to quicken the conscience by the holiness of God, to
feed the mind with the truth of God, to purge the imagination by the
beauty of God, to open the heart to the love of God, to devote the will
to the purpose of God. All this is gathered up in that emotion which
most cleanses us from selfishness because it is the most selfless of all
emotions—adoration.

WILLIAM TEMPLE: *The Hope of a New World*

The Bent World

The world is charged with the grandeur of God.
  It will flame out, like shining from shook foil;
  It gathers to a greatness, like the ooze of oil
Crushed. Why do men then now not reck his rod?
Generations have trod, have trod, have trod;
  And all is seared with trade; bleared, smeared with toil;
  And wears man's smudge and shares man's smell: the soil
Is bare now, nor can foot feel, being shod.

And for all this, nature is never spent;
  There lives the dearest freshness deep down things;
And though the last lights off the black West went
  Oh, morning, at the brown brink eastward, springs—
Because the Holy Ghost over the bent
  World broods with warm breast and with ah! bright wings.

GERARD MANLEY HOPKINS

Bibliography of Principal Sources

BIBLIOGRAPHY OF PRINCIPAL SOURCES

Publishers' names are supplied for most current books. For older standard works, for those sometimes available in several editions, and a few
perhaps only available in libraries, publisher data is not supplied.

Augustine (St.). *Confessions.*
Ausubel, Nathan (ed.). *A Treasury of Jewish Folklore.* New York: Crown
Publishers.

Baillie, John. *Natural Science and the Spiritual Life.* New York: Scribner.
Bayne, Stephen F., Jr. "God is the Teacher," *The Christian Idea of Educa-
tion.* New Haven: Yale Univ. Press.
_____ "Understanding Europe from the Inside," *Schools and Scholarship.*
New Haven: Yale Univ. Press.
Berdyaev, Nicolas. *The Meaning of History.* New York: Meridian Books.
_____ *The Realm of Spirit and the Realm of Caesar.* New York: Harper
& Row.
Bettenson, H. (ed.). *The Early Christian Fathers.* London and New York:
Oxford Univ. Press.
Blackburn, E. A. (ed.). *A Treasury of the Kingdom.* London and New
York: Oxford Univ. Press.
Bonhoeffer, Dietrich. *Temptation.* New York: Macmillan.
Buber, Martin. *Eclipse of God.* New York: Harper & Row.
_____ *Good and Evil.* New York: Scribner.
_____ *I and Thou.* New York: Scribner.
Bunyan, John. *The Saint's Privilege and Profit.*
Butterfield, Herbert. *Christianity in History.* New York: Scribner.

Calvin, John. "Instruction in Faith," *Great Voices of the Reformation.*
New York: Modern Library, Random House.
Casserley, J. V. L. *The Bent World.* London and New York: Oxford Univ.
Press.
_____ *Graceful Reason.* New York: Seabury Press.
Chesterton, G. K. *The Everlasting Man.* New York: Image Books, Double-
day.
Coleridge, Hartley. *Poems.*
Coulson, C. A. *Science and Christian Belief.* Chapel Hill: Univ. of North
Carolina Press.

D'Arcy, Martin C. *No Absent God.* New York: Harper & Row.
Desbiens, Jean-Paul. *Les Insolences du Frère Untel.*

Donne, John. *Donne's Sermons: Selected Passages* (L. P. Smith, ed.). London and New York: Oxford Univ. Press.
———— *Poems.*
———— *The Showing Forth of Christ* (Selected Sermons ed. by Edmund Fuller). New York: Harper & Row.
Dostoyevsky, Fyodor. *The Brothers Karamazov.*

Eliot, T. S. *Murder in the Cathedral.* New York: Harcourt, Brace & World.
———— *Selected Essays.* New York: Harcourt, Brace & World.

Fitch, Robert Elliot. *The Odyssey of the Self-Centered Self.* New York: Harcourt, Brace & World.
Fosdick, H. E. (ed.). *Great Voices of the Reformation.* New York: Modern Library, Random House.
Fuller, Edmund (ed.). *The Christian Idea of Education.* New Haven: Yale Univ. Press.
———— *Schools and Scholarship.* New Haven: Yale Univ. Press.
———— *The Showing Forth of Christ.* New York: Harper & Row.
Fuller, Thomas. *Good Thoughts in Bad Times.*

Gary, Romain. *The Ski Bum.* New York: Harper & Row.
Greene, Graham. *The Labyrinthine Ways.* New York: Viking Press.

Hammarskjöld, Dag. *Markings.* New York: Alfred A. Knopf.
Hedley, George. *The Superstitions of the Irreligious.* New York: Macmillan.
Heim, Karl. *Christian Faith and Natural Science.* New York: Harper & Row.
———— *The Transformation of the Scientific World View.* New York: Harper & Row.
Herbert, George. *Poems.*
Heschel, Abraham. *God in Search of Man.* New York: Farrar, Straus & Giroux.
Hopkins, Gerard Manley. *Poems.* London and New York: Oxford Univ. Press.

Kirk, Russell. *The Intemperate Professor.* Baton Rouge: Louisiana State University Press.

Lawrence (Brother). *The Practice of the Presence of God.*
Lewis, C. S. *The Problem of Pain.* New York: Macmillan.
———— *Surprised by Joy.* New York: Harcourt, Brace & World.
———— *The World's Last Night.* New York: Harcourt, Brace & World.
Luther, Martin. "Concerning Christian Liberty," *Great Voices of the Reformation.* New York: Modern Library, Random House.

Maritain, Jacques, *Approaches to God*. New York: Harper & Row.
Mary Immaculate, Sister. *The Tree and the Master*. New York: Random House.
Mauriac, François. *Cain, Where is Your Brother?* New York: Coward-McCann.
Merton, Thomas. *Seasons of Celebration*. New York: Farrar, Straus & Giroux.
Milford, T. R. *Foolishness to the Greeks*. New York: Seabury Press.
Milton, John. *Areopagitica*.

Niebuhr, Reinhold. *The Self and the Dramas of History*. New York: Scribner.
———— "The Two Sources of Western Culture," *The Christian Idea of Education*. New Haven: Yale Univ. Press.

Pascal, Blaise. *Pensées*.
Paton, Alan. "The Person in Community," *The Christian Idea of Education*. New Haven: Yale Univ. Press.
Pollard, William G. *The Cosmic Drama*. New York: Faculty Papers, National Council of the Protestant Episcopal Church.
———— *Physicist and Christian*. New York: Seabury Press.

Roberts, David E. *The Grandeur and Misery of Man*. London and New York: Oxford Univ. Press.
Roethke, Theodore. *Collected Poems*. New York: Doubleday.
———— *On the Poet and His Craft*. Seattle: Univ. of Washington Press.

Sayers, Dorothy L. *Creed or Chaos*. London: Methuen.
———— *The Mind of the Maker*. New York: Meridian Books.
Shaw, G. B. *Saint Joan*. New York: Dodd, Mead & Co.

Teilhard de Chardin, Pierre. *The Divine Milieu*. New York: Harper & Row.
Temple, William. *Christ in His Church*.
———— *The Hope of a New World*.
———— *Readings in St. John's Gospel*. New York: St. Martin's Press.
———— *The Universality of Christ*.
Tillich, Paul. *Biblical Religion and the Search for Ultimate Reality*. Chicago: Univ. of Chicago Press.
———— *Love, Power, and Justice*, London and New York: Oxford Univ. Press.
———— *The New Being*. New York: Scribner.
———— *The Shaking of the Foundations*. New York: Scribner.
Traherne, Thomas. *Centuries of Meditations*. New York: Farrar, Straus & Giroux.

Underhill, Evelyn. *An Anthology of the Love of God*. New York: David McKay.

Updike, John. *Telephone Poles and Other Poems*. New York: Alfred A. Knopf.

Vale, Eugene. *Chaos Below Heaven*. New York: Doubleday.

—————— *The Thirteenth Apostle*. New York: Scribner.

Walsh, Chad. *Behold the Glory*. New York: Harper & Row.

—————— *The Psalm of Christ*. Philadelphia: Westminster Press.

Ward Barbara. *Faith and Freedom*. New York: W. W. Norton.

Weil, Simone. *The Need for Roots*. New York: Putnam.

—————— *Waiting for God*. New York: Putnam.

Whale, J. S. *Christian Doctrine*. Cambridge: Cambridge Univ. Press.

Whitehead, A. N. *Science and the Modern World*. New York: Mentor Books, New American Library.

Wycliffe, John. "The Poor Caitiff," *Great Voices of the Reformation*. New York: Modern Library, Random House.

Index of Authors

INDEX OF AUTHORS